Australian Shepherd
Miniature American Shepherd

PAULA MCDERMID PHOTO

BREEDER / PHOTOGRAPHER MELISSA ZOBELL

FCI Breed Standards detailed in 238 photos

FCI Rassenstandards in 238 detaillierten Fotos

ENGLISH and DEUTSCH 🇬🇧 🇩🇪

Paula McDermid • Claudia Bosselmann • Inga Cerbule

"I read this book from cover to cover and find it to be an accurate and needed comparison of the Australian Shepherd and Miniature American Shepherd breed standards. I appreciated the explanations for each section of the standards. The pictures clearly show the desirable traits and any breed differences. This book should be read and used as a reference by both judges and breeders."

Sue Ritter. Legacy Australian Shepherds and Miniature American Shepherds since 1980. Hall of Fame breeder, judge's educator and mentor, current President and former Vice-President of the AKC parent club Miniature American Shepherd Club of the USA.

"Ich habe dieses Buch von der ersten bis zur letzten Seite gelesen und finde, dass es ein genauer und notwendiger Vergleich der Rassestandards des Australian Shepherd und des Miniature American Shepherd ist. Ich schätzte die Erklärungen zu jedem Abschnitt der Standards. Die Bilder zeigen deutlich die erwünschten Eigenschaften und alle Rassenunterschiede. Dieses Buch sollte von Richtern und Züchtern gelesen und als Nachschlagewerk verwendet werden."

Sue Ritter. Legacy Australian Shepherds und Miniature American Shepherds seit 1980. Hall of Fame-Züchterin, Richterausbilderin und Mentorin, derzeitige Präsidentin und ehemalige Vizepräsidentin des AKC-Mutterclubs Miniature American Shepherd Club of the USA.

Book design by Paula McDermid and translated by Claudia Bosselmann. Translation of the FCI Australian Shepherd breed standard from English to German by Dr. J-M. Paschoud and Frau R. Binder, supplement by Christina Bailey. Translation of the FCI Miniature American Shepherd breed standard from English to German by Firma Skrivanek.

First printing November 2021
Updated April 2024
ISBN 978-0-9975534-5-1

Buchgestaltung von Paula McDermid und Übersetzt von Claudia Bosselmann. Übersetzung des FCI-Rassestandards für den Australian Shepherd aus dem Englischen ins Deutsche von Dr. J-M. Paschoud und Frau R. Binder, Ergänzung durch Christina Bailey. Übersetzung des FCI-Rassestandards für den Amerikanischen Miniaturschäferhund aus dem Englischen ins Deutsche von der Firma Skrivanek.

Erstdruck November 2021
Aktualisiert April 2024
ISBN 978-0-9975534-5-1

Contents / Inhalt

A conformation dog show is not a comparison of one dog to another. It's a comparison of each dog to the *breed standard*.

Eine Hundeausstellung ist kein Vergleich eines Hundes mit einem anderen.
Es ist ein Vergleich jedes Hundes mit dem *Rassestandard.*

What you will learn

- To identify correct breed type and characteristics.

Why that's important

- Influence breeding decisions of exhibitors by rewarding the best representatives of the breed, thereby improving the breed.

- Improve quality of judging.

- Demonstrate your knowledge to exhibitors.

Breed Standards are very similar

- The Australian Shepherd and Miniature American Shepherd breed standards are very similar. In this presentation the differences are highlighted.

Was Sie lernen werden

- Den richtigen Rassetyp und den richtigen Merkmale zu identifizieren.

Warum das wichtig ist

- Beeinflussen Sie Zuchtentscheidungen der Aussteller, indem Sie die besten Vertreter der Rasse belohnen und so die Rasse verbessern.

- Verbessern Sie die Qualität der Beurteilung.

- Zeigen Sie Ihr Wissen vor Ausstellern.

Die Rassestandards sind sehr ähnlich

- Die Rassestandards für Australian Shepherd und Miniature American Shepherd sind sehr ähnlich. In dieser Präsentation werden die Unterschiede hervorgehoben.

As the standards were written, Aussies and MAS should have the conformation to be able to function as stockdogs and compete successfully at high levels in canine sports. However, when they have too much bone or coat, when they have incorrect or unbalanced angles, they can't perform the work for which they were bred. Judges need to adhere to the standards and encourage breeders to steer away from exaggerated traits which can predispose dogs to pain and injury.

Als die Standards geschrieben wurden, sollten Aussies und MAS das Exterieur haben, um als Arbeitshunde funktionieren und erfolgreich auf hohem Niveau im Hundesport konkurrieren zu können. Das Problem ist, wenn sie nicht die richtigen Winkelungen haben oder zu viel Winkelung, schlimmer noch nicht balancierte Winkel, sind sie einfach nicht in der Lage dazu. Richter müssen sich an den Standard halten und Züchter ermutigen, sich von übertriebenen Merkmalen fernzuhalten, die Hunde oft für Schmerzen und Verletzungen anfällig machen.

DORIEN VOGELAAR PHOTOGRAPHY

HOLLY REGINA PRESS PHOTO

RICK PITTMAN PHOTO

Bred to be Athletic

Ein athletische Hunderasse

Aussies and MAS are intelligent working dogs of strong herding and guarding instincts

- They are loyal companions and have the stamina to work all day.

- With an even disposition, they are good natured, seldom quarrelsome.

- They may be somewhat reserved during initial meetings. They are not shy or timid; they are cautious but will accept unfamiliar people who approach quietly. When judging Aussies and MAS, it is best to avoid leaning over the dog.

VERHALTEN UND TEMPERAMENT

Aussies und MAS sind intelligente Arbeitshunde mit starkem Hüte- und Bewachungsinstinkt

- Sie sind treue Begleiter und haben die Ausdauer, den ganzen Tag zu arbeiten.

- Bei ausgeglichener Veranlagung sind sie gutmütig, selten streitsüchtig.

- Sie können während der ersten Treffen etwas zurückhaltend sein. Sie sind nicht scheu oder ängstlich; sie sind vorsichtig, akzeptieren aber unbekannte Menschen, die sich ruhig nähern. Beim Beurteilen von Aussies und MAS sollte man es am besten vermeiden, sich über den Hund zu beugen.

ROCK: Livestock herding

BRUCE: Best friend and protector

Strong herding and guarding instincts. Good-natured, devoted, loyal.

Starker Hüte- und Wachinstinkt. Gutmütig, hingebungsvoll und treu.

Moderation is the single most important quality of these breeds

Their purpose as stockdogs requires moderate structure:

- for quick acceleration to turn back livestock
- for agility to dodge horns and kicking hooves
- to alter gait instantly to outmaneuver livestock
- and for strength and stamina to work all day over rough ground during rain, sleet, snow and under hot sun.

Aussies and MAS are very popular as canine sport dogs and family companions. They require the same moderate structure as stockdogs to play, compete successfully and to avoid injuries.

WARUM MODERATE STRUKTUR?

Eine moderate Struktur ist die wichtigste Eigenschaft dieser Rassen

Ihr Zweck als Arbeitshunde erfordert eine moderate Struktur:

- für eine schnelle Beschleunigung, um das Vieh zurückzubringen
- für maximale Agilität, um Hörnern und Hufen auszuweichen
- den Gang sofort zu ändern, um das Vieh auszumanövrieren
- und für Kraft und Ausdauer, um den ganzen Tag auf unebenem Boden bei Regen, Graupel, Schnee und unter heißer Sonne zu arbeiten.

Aussies und MAS sind als Sporthunde und Familienhunde sehr beliebt. Sie erfordern die gleiche moderate Struktur wie Arbeitshunde, um zu spielen, erfolgreich im Wettbewerb zu konkurrieren und Verletzungen zu vermeiden.

DUKE: Livestock herding

TURBO: Disc dog

RIBBON: Playing ball

SMOOCH: Agility

The moderate structure and athletic ability necessary for livestock herding are also necessary for other working tasks and many popular dog sports.

Die für die Viehhaltung notwendige moderate Struktur und athletische Fähigkeit sind auch für andere Arbeitsaufgaben und viele Hundesportarten notwendig.

Aussies and MAS need to be agile, structurally sound and totally functional

Avoid exaggerated features that are atypical and undesirable for these moderate working breeds such as:

- domed head with exaggerated stop and round eyes or head too narrow and snipey
- excess skin around eyes and lips
- large, heavy, low-set ears with no lift
- excess coat and excess bone, or too little bone
- chest too wide, too narrow or shallow
- low on leg
- Sloping topline and excess rear angulation. These traits are structurally unstable for working stockdogs.
- Extreme, flashy sidegait is an artificial gait designed to win in the show ring but is not a functional working gait.

Preserving the integrity of the breeds means avoiding extremes and returning to moderate.

AUFMERKSAM, ANIMIERT, GESCHMEIDIG, AGIL

Aussies und MAS müssen agil, strukturell solide und absolut funktional sein

Vermeiden Sie übertriebene Merkmale, die für diese gemäßigten Arbeitsrassen untypisch und unerwünscht sind.

- gewölbter Kopf mit übertriebenem Stop und runden Augen oder Kopf zu schmal und spitz.
- überschüssige Haut um Augen und Lippen
- große, schwere, tief angesetzte Ohren ohne Hub
- überschüssiges Fell und zu viel oder zu wenig Knochen
- brust zu breit, zu schmal oder zu flach
- zu kurze Beinlänge
- Abfallende Oberlinie und übermäßige hintere Winkelung. Diese Merkmale sind für Arbeitshunde strukturell instabil.
- Das extreme, auffällige Seitengangwerk (Flying Trot) ist eine künstliche Gangart, die entwickelt wurde, um im Showring zu gewinnen, aber keine funktionierende Arbeitsgangart.

Um die Integrität der Rassen zu bewahren, bedeutet es, Extreme zu vermeiden und zum Moderaten zurückzukehren.

DOC: Livestock herding

SUSAN SEVERNS PHOTOGRAPHY

BLOOM: Agility

GINGER & BLACK PHOTOGRAPHY

Moderate structure is necessary for quick acceleration and the flexibility to maneuver instantly in any direction.

Moderate Struktur für schnelle Beschleunigung und Flexibilität, um sofort in jede Richtung zu manövrieren.

Aussies and MAS work hard at many jobs

Because of their high intelligence and eagerness to learn, they are prized for the work they perform.

- Herding, ranch and farm dogs
- Search and Rescue
- Crisis response
- Police work and narcotic detection
- Canine defense
- Seeing-eye dogs
- Hearing-ear dogs
- Utility dogs for the handicapped
- Therapy dogs
- Seizure detection dogs
- and more

VIELSEITIG

Aussies und MAS arbeiten hart in vielen Jobs

- Aufgrund ihrer hohen Intelligenz und Lernbereitschaft werden sie für ihre Leistung geschätzt
- Hüte-, Ranch- und Farmhunde
- Such- und Rettungshunde
- Einsatz in Krisensituationen
- Polizeiarbeit und Suche nach Betäubungsmitteln
- Schutzdienst
- Blindenhunde
- Hunde für Taube
- Gebrauchshunde für Behinderte
- Therapiehunde
- Epilepsiewarnhunde
- und mehr

LOLA: Water rescue training

JINDRICH HANACEK PHOTOGRAPHY

MAC: Canine defense

MICHELLE BESTER PHOTOGRAPHY

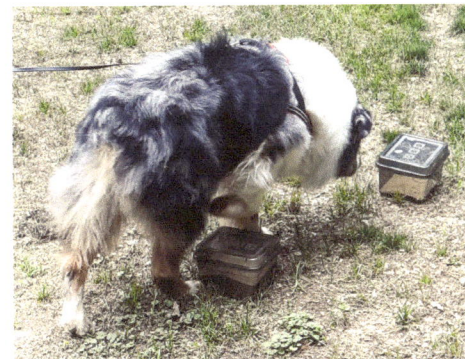

GRIFF: Scent detection

KAY MARKS PHOTO

MCGYVER: Search and rescue

RICK STEIN PHOTO

ANDREW: Livestock herding

BECKY PARKER, DALLY UP PHOTOGRAPHY

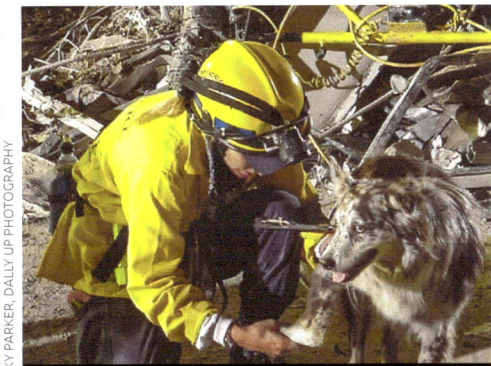

HAWK: Crisis response, 911 World Trade Towers

MISSOURI TASK FORCE 1 PHOTO

(Links nach rechts) 1. Wasserrettung 2. Schutzdienst 3. Geruchserkennung 4. Suche & Rettung 5. Viehzucht 6. Krisenreaktion 911 World Trade Towers

Aussies and MAS excel in canine sports

Moderate structure along with superior intelligence and trainability make them truly versatile.

- Agility
- Flyball
- Frisbee
- Rally
- Obedience
- Dock diving
- Trick dogs
- Freestyle dancing
- Sled racing and ski-jouring
- All-around companion

They can do all this and more.

VIELSEITIG

Aussies und MAS zeichnen sich im Hundesport aus

Moderate Struktur zusammen mit überlegener Intelligenz und Trainierbarkeit machen sie wirklich vielseitig.

- Agility
- Flyball
- Frisbee
- Rallye
- Obedience
- Dog Diving
- Trick Dog
- Dog Dance
- Schlittenrennen und Skijouring
- Allround-Begleiter

Sie können all dies und noch mehr.

APPLEDORE TEAM: Dog sled

DIANA MINGALIEVA PHOTO

TESS: Disc dog

LINDSEY THOMPSON PHOTOGRAPHY

ZIGGY: Flyball

JIM GEISER PHOTO

NEYLA: Agility

CLAUDIA BOSSELMANN PHOTO

BLIZZ: Agility

DOREN VOGELAAR PHOTOGRAPHY

1. Hundeschlitten 2. Disc Dog 3. Flyball 4. Agility 5. Agility

Wie das

Wie das

MODERATER KNOCHENBAU UND SUBSTANZ

Males reflect masculinity without coarseness.

Wie das. Rüden strahlen Maskulinität aus, ohne grob zu wirken.

Bitches appear feminine without being slight of bone.

Wie das: Hündinnen erscheinen feminin, ohne zu leicht zu wirken.

Nicht das

Nicht das

Not THAT — Nicht das QUADRAT **SQUARE**

Like THIS — Wie das RICHTIG **CORRECT**

Not THAT — Nicht das ZU LANG **TOO LONG**

Body Length: AUSSIES: Measure from breastbone to rear of thigh. **MAS:** Measure from point of the shoulder to the point of the buttock. The body length is slightly greater than the height from the highest point of the withers to the ground, as a ratio of 10:9. If the body appears too long, either the ribcage or the loin is too long. From withers to base of tail, correct proportions should be 50% rib cage, 25% loin, 25% croup. Use your hands to verify.

Körperlänge: AUSSIES: Von der Brustbeinspitze zum Sitzbeinhöcker gemessen. **MAS:** Vom Buggelenk bis zum Sitzbeinhöcker. Die Körperlänge ist etwas größer als die Höhe vom höchsten Widerristpunkt bis zum Boden im Verhältnis 10:9. Wenn der Körper zu lang erscheint, ist entweder der Brustkorb oder die Lende zu lang. Vom Widerrist bis zum Rutenansatz sollten die richtigen Proportionen 50 % Brustkorb, 25 % Lende, 25 % Kruppe betragen. Verwenden Sie Ihre Hände, um dies zu überprüfen.

Like THIS

Not THAT

Correct / Beine haben die richtige Höhe

Legs too short / Beine sind zu kurz

Leg Length: Equidistant from elbow to ground and elbow to withers.

Beinlänge: Gleicher Abstand vom Ellbogen zum Boden und vom Ellbogen zum Widerrist.

- Medium size.
- Solidly built with moderate bone.
- Muscular without cloddiness.

PROPORTIONEN ETWAS LÄNGER ALS HOCH

- Mittlere Größe.
- Kräftig gebaut mit moderatem Knochenbau.
- Muskulös, ohne jedoch massig zu wirken.

Like
THIS

Wie das

AUSTRALIAN SHEPHERDS

AUSSIES:
Preferred heights
No size disqualification
MALES
Maximum 23 inches (58 cm)
Minimum 20 inches (51 cm)
FEMALES
Maximum 21 inches (53 cm)
Minimum 18 inches (46 cm)

AUSSIES:
Bevorzugte Größe
Keine Größendisqualifikation
RÜDEN
Maximal 23 Zoll (58 cm)
Mindestens 20 Zoll (51 cm)
HÜNDINNEN
Maximal 21 Zoll (53 cm)
Mindestens 18 Zoll (46 cm)

The quality of the dog is more important than a slight deviation from the ideal size.

Bei der Beurteilung der Größe ist die Qualität des Hundes wichtiger als eine leichte Abweichung von der Idealgröße.

MINIATURE AMERICAN SHEPHERDS

MAS:
Designated heights
DISQUALIFICATION: OVER OR UNDER SIZE
MALES
Maximum 18 inches (46 cm)
Minimum 14 inches (35.5 cm)
FEMALES
Maximum 17 inches (43.5 cm)
Minimum 13 inches (33 cm)

MAS:
Vorgesehene Höhen
DISQUALIFIKATION: ÜBER- ODER UNTERGRÖßE
RÜDEN
Maximal 18 Zoll (46 cm)
Mindestens 14 Zoll (35,5 cm)
HÜNDINNEN
Maximal 17 Zoll (43,5 cm)
Mindestens 13 Zoll (33 cm)

A healthy weight will be based on individual height, gender, and substance.

Ein gesundes Gewicht wird auf der individuellen Größe, dem Geschlecht und der Substanz basieren.

AUSSIE: Large male 23" (58 cm)
AUSSIE: Großer Rüde 23" (58 cm)
AUSSIE: Small female 18" (46 cm)
AUSSIE: Kleine Hündin 18" (46 cm)
MAS: Large male 18" (46cm)
MAS: Großer Rüde 18" (46cm)
MAS: Small female 13" (33 cm)
MAS: Kleine Hündin 13" (33 cm)

AMBER JADE ANNENSEN PHOTOGRAPHY

Head
Strong and Expressive

Kopf
Kräftig und Ausdrucksvoll

DEFINITION OF CLEAN CUT

Chiseled outline
Neat and tidy with no loose skin

AUSSIES AND MAS:

- Clean cut, strong and dry
- Overall size should be in proportion to the body.

Skull

- **AUSSIES:** Top flat to slightly domed.
- **MAS:** Flat to slightly round. (smooth down hair to see true shape)
- May show a slight occipital protuberance.
- Length and width are equal.

Stop

- **AUSSIES:** Moderate, well-defined.
- **MAS:** Moderate but defined. Abrupt stops are undesirable. Keep in mind that the stop's angle must allow for a kick to glance off.

SAUBERER SCHNITT DES KOPFES

DEFINITION VON CLEAN CUT

Saubere Umrisslinien
Saubere und trocken ohne lose Haut

AUSSIES UND MAS:

- Saubere Umrisslinie, kräftig und trocken
- Der Kopf steht in einem guten Größenverhältnis zum Körper.

Schädel

- **AUSSIES:** Das Schädeldach ist flach bis leicht gewölbt.
- **MAS:** Das Schädeldach ist flach bis mäßig rund
- Der Hinterhauptstachel kann etwas sichtbar sein.
- Die Schädellänge entspricht der Schädelbreite.

Stopp

- **AUSSIES:** Moderat, gut definiert.
- **MAS:** Mäßig, jedoch definiert ausgebildet. Abrupte Stopps sind unerwünscht. Denken Sie daran, dass der Winkel des Stopps ein Abprallen eines Tritts ermöglichen muss.

Diese sind richtig

Like THIS

Wie das

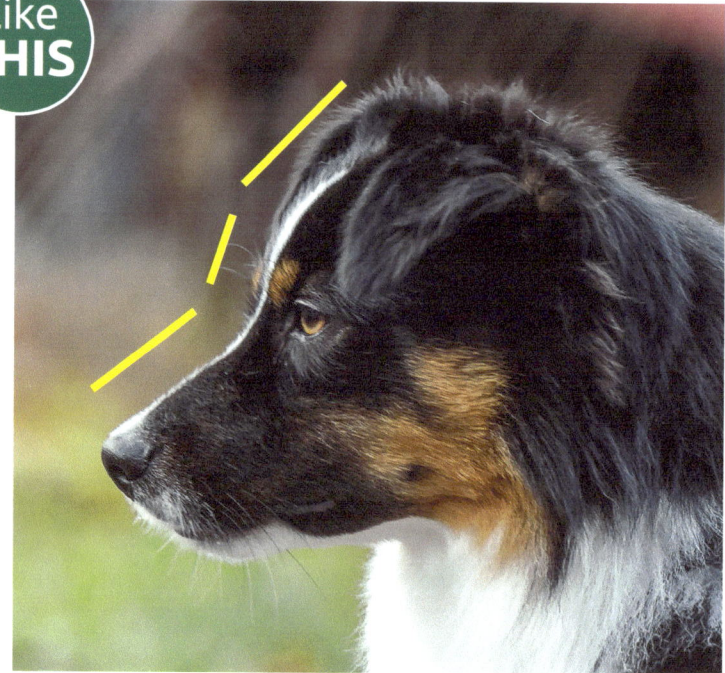

Like THIS

Wie das

Correct

AUSSIES: Top flat to slightly domed. It may show a slight occipital protuberance. Viewed from the side, the topline of the back skull and muzzle form parallel planes (smooth down hair to check).

MAS: Viewed from the side, the muzzle and the top line of the crown are slightly oblique to each other, with the front of the crown on a slight angle downward toward the nose. The stop is moderate but defined.

KORREKTE KOPFLINIEN

AUSSIES: Oben flach bis leicht gewölbt. Es kann eine leichte Hinterhauptsprotuberanz aufweisen. Von der Seite betrachtet bilden die Oberlinie des Hinterkopfes und die Schnauze parallele Ebenen (zur Kontrolle Haare glätten).

MAS: Von der Seite betrachtet stehen die Schnauze und die obere Linie des Scheitels leicht schräg zueinander, wobei die Vorderseite des Scheitels zur Nase hin leicht nach unten geneigt ist. Der Stopp ist mäßig, jedoch definiert ausgebildet.

Not
THAT

Nicht das

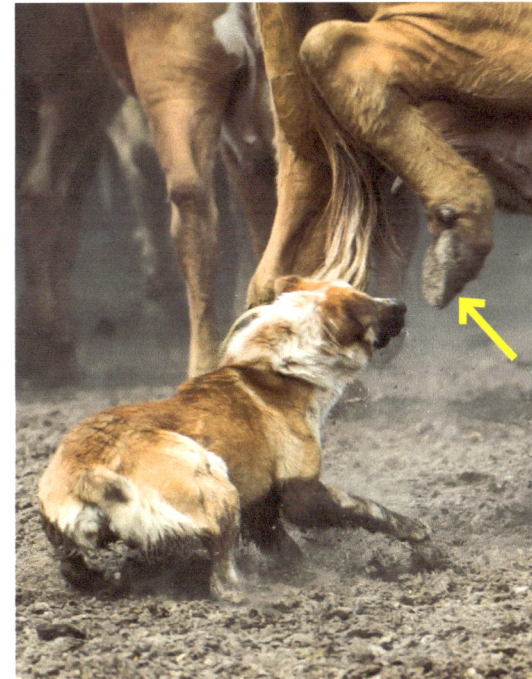

The dog was kicked by a cow and received a glancing blow. The skin was scraped, but his eye was not damaged. If this dog's stop had been steep, like the dog at left, the kick would have been a direct blow to his forehead.

Der Hund wurde von einer Kuh mit einem Huf getroffen, aber der Tritt streifte nur den Kopf. Die Haut wurde aufgeschürft, das Auge aber nicht verletzt. Hätte dieser Hund einen steilen Stopp, wie der Hund ganz links, hätte ihn der Tritt mit voller Wucht an der Stirn getroffen.

Exaggeration

A domed skull and exaggerated stop may catch a flying hoof, increasing the risk of severe head injury. Correct head planes and moderate stop allow a hoof to glance off the head.

Why should exaggeration be avoided?

Correct bone structure helps protect the skull and brain from a blow to the head and can reduce the risk of injury to sight, hearing, and scent. Correct head structure is a safety factor and an essential breed characteristic.

GEWÖLBTER KOPF UND ÜBERTRIEBENER STOPP

Übertreibung

Ein gewölbter Schädel und ein übertriebener Stopp können einen fliegenden Huf abfangen und erhöhen das Risiko schwerer Kopfverletzungen. Korrekte Kopfebenen und ein moderater Stopp ermöglichen es einem Huf, vom Kopf abzuprallen.

Warum sollte Übertreibung vermieden werden?

Die richtige Knochenstruktur schützt den Schädel und das Gehirn vor einem Schlag auf den Kopf und kann das Risiko von Seh-, Hör- und Geruchsverletzungen verringern. Der richtige Anatomie des Kopfes ist ein Sicherheitsfaktor und ein wesentliches Rassemerkmal.

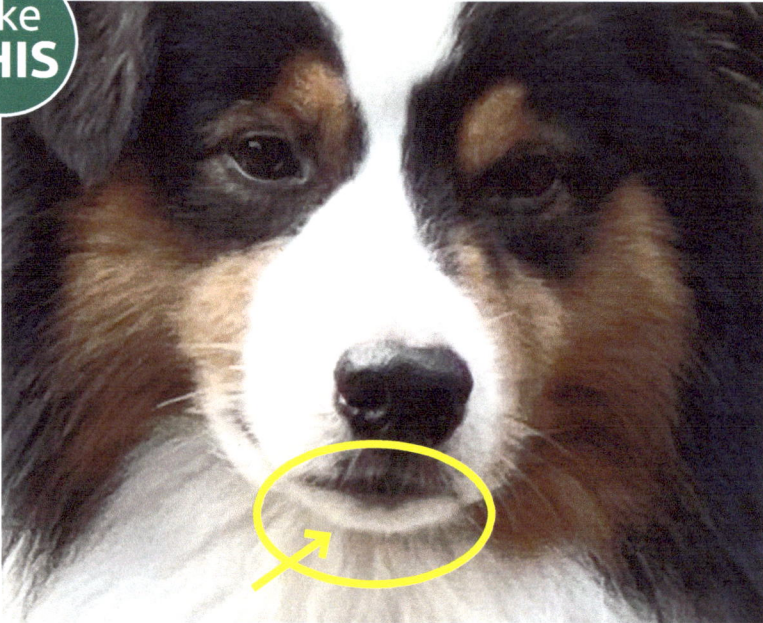

CHERYL NAKAKURA PHOTO

Wie das

DEFINITION OF STRONG HEAD

- Solid bone structure.
- Full muzzle with deep underjaw that provides strong bone to anchor teeth.
- For ranch dogs this is necessary for gripping stock and to minimize injury from the impact of a kick. It's also important for competitors in canine sports and everyday life.

KRÄFTIGER KOPF UND UNTERKIEFER

DEFINITION KRÄFTIGER KOPF

- Solide Knochenstruktur.
- Volle Schnauze mit tiefem Unterkiefer, der starken Knochen bietet, um die Zähne zu verankern.
- Für Ranchhunde ist dies notwendig, um das Vieh zu greifen und Verletzungen durch den Aufprall eines Tritts zu minimieren. Es ist auch wichtig für Wettkämpfer im Hundesport und im Alltag.

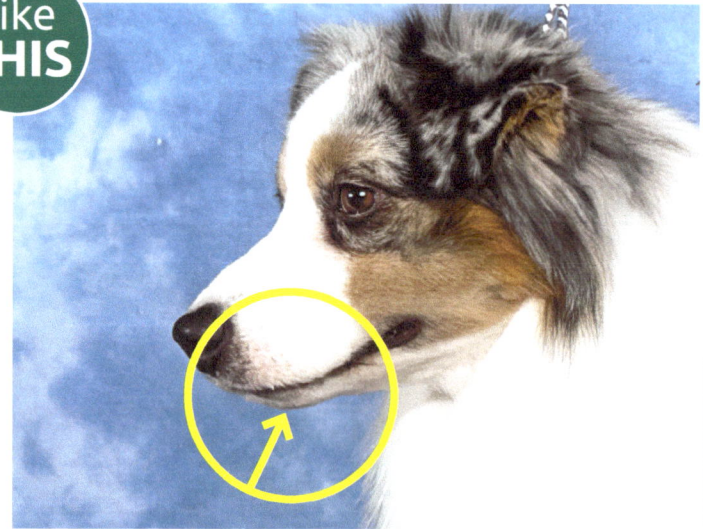

JC DOG PHOTOGRAPHY.NET

Wie das

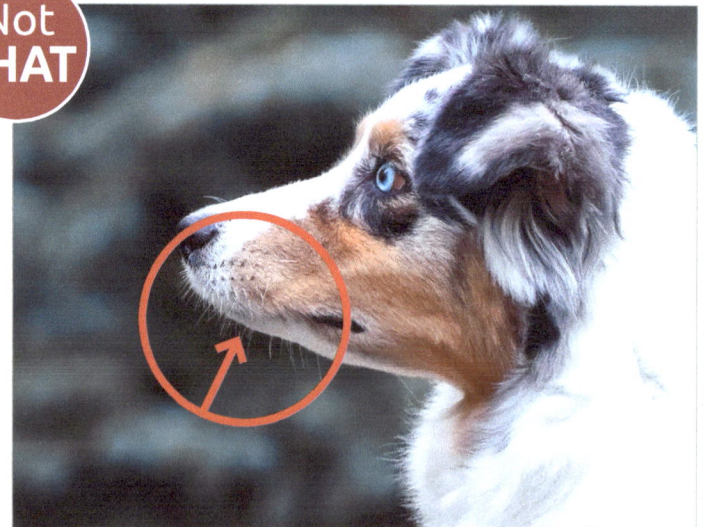

DENIS NATA PHOTO / SHUTTERSTOCK

Nicht das

PAULA MCDERMID PHOTO

AMBER JADE AANENSEN PHOTOGRAPHY

Wie das

Muzzle length

AUSSIES: Equal in length or slightly shorter than the back skull.

MAS: Length is equal to the length of the crown.

Wie das

Muzzle shape

AUSSIES: The muzzle tapers little from base to nose and is rounded at the tip.

MAS: The muzzle is of medium width and depth and tapers gradually to a rounded tip without appearing heavy, square, snipy, or loose.

KOPFPROPORTIONEN UND FANG

Länge des Fangs

AUSSIES: Der Fang ist gleich lang oder etwas kürzer als der Schädel.

MAS: Die Länge entspricht der Länge des Oberkopfes.

Form des Fangs

AUSSIES: Der Fang verjüngt sich nur wenig vom Ansatz bis zum Nasenschwamm und ist am Ende abgerundet.

MAS: Der Fang ist von mittlerer Breite und Tiefe, verjüngt sich graduell zu einer abgerundeten Spitze, ohne schwer, quadratisch, spitz oder lose zu wirken.

EYES

No loose skin around the eyes

- The skin around the eyes should be snug for best protection of the eyeballs. It creates the characteristic almond shape.

- Eyelids shield the eyes from dust, wind, and debris.

- When the skin of the head is loose or the lower eyelid muscles are weak, the lower eyelid can droop down and roll away from the eye, exposing the delicate inner eyelid tissue. This is called a **haw or ectropion**.

WHY is loose skin around the eyes undesirable?

Drooping lower eyelids (haws/ectropion) expose the delicate inner eyelid tissue, which can result in painful corneal inflammation, corneal scarring, and impaired vision. Haws can trap seeds, dirt, and debris that can injure the eyes. They also detract from correct expression.

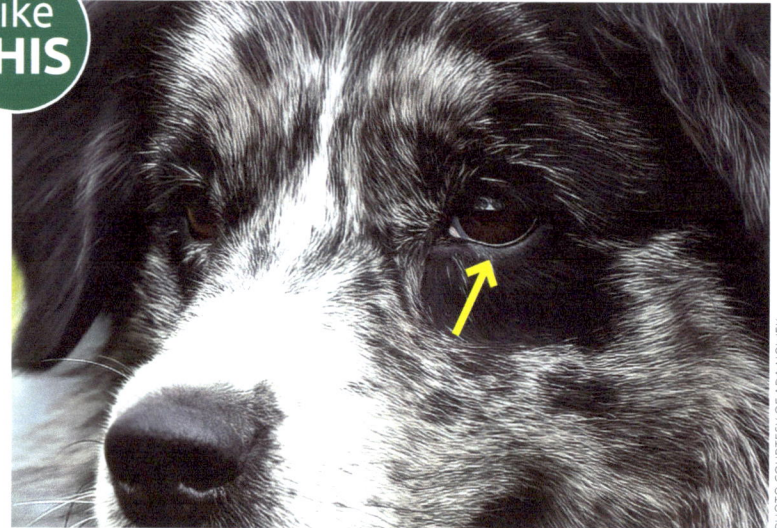

Wie das

TROCKENER KOPF

AUGEN

Keine lose Haut um die Augen

- Die Haut um die Augen sollte eng anliegen, um die Augäpfel optimal zu schützen. Dadurch entsteht die charakteristische Mandelform.

- Augenlider schützen die Augen vor Staub, Wind und Schmutz.

- Wenn die Haut am Kopf schlaff ist oder die Unterlidmuskeln schwach sind, kann das Unterlid herabhängen und vom Auge wegrollen, wodurch das empfindliche innere Lidgewebe freigelegt wird. Dies wird als **Haw** oder **Ektropium** bezeichnet.

WARUM ist schlaffe Haut um die Augen unerwünscht?

- Hängende Unterlider (Haws/ Ektropium) legen das empfindliche innere Augenlidgewebe frei, was zu schmerzhaften Hornhautentzündungen, Hornhautvernarbungen und Sehstörungen führen kann. Haws können Samen, Schmutz und Ablagerungen einschließen, die die Augen verletzen können. Außerdem beeinträchtigen sie den korrekten Ausdruck.

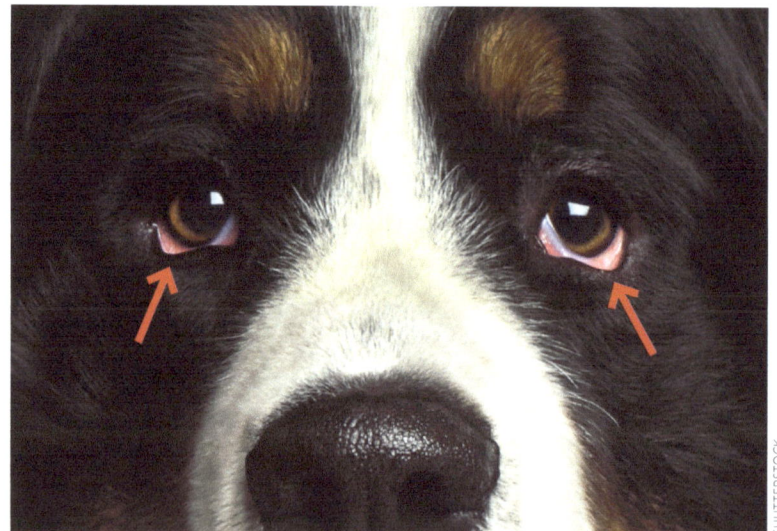

Nicht das

MOUTH
No extra or loose skin around mouth

- Straight, clean lipline created by tight lips.
- Upper and lower lips should meet and fit smoothly together all the way around the muzzle.

WHY?

- Minimizes risk of lips being snagged and torn during conflict with other animals.
- Detracts from correct breed type.

TROCKENER KOPF

FANG
Keine zusätzliche oder lose Haut um den Fang

- Gerade, saubere Lippenlinie durch straffe Lippen.
- Ober- und Unterlippe sollten sich treffen und glatt zusammenfügen.

WARUM?

- Minimiert das Risiko, dass die Lippe bei Konflikten mit anderen Tieren hängen bleibt oder reißt.
- Ist für die Rasse nicht korrekt.

Like THIS

Wie das

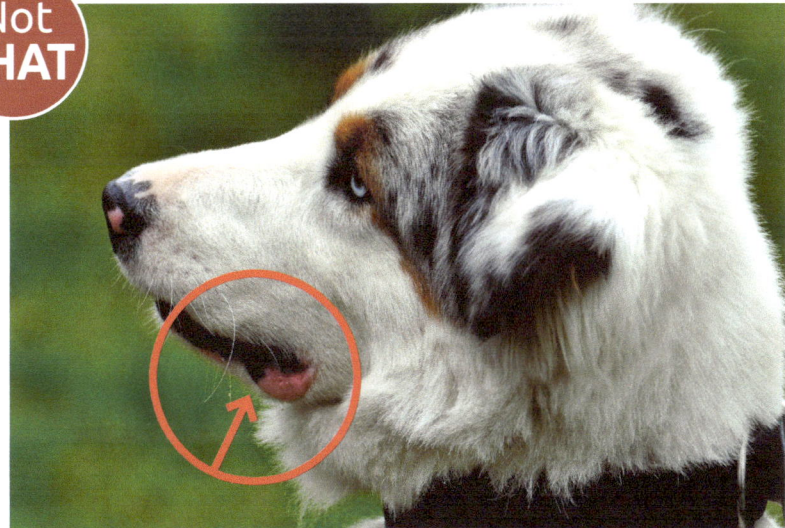

Not THAT

Nicht das

AUSSIES: A full complement of strong white teeth should meet in a scissors bite or may meet in a pincer bite.

DISQUALIFICATION: Undershot. Overshot by more than ⅛ inch (0.3 cm). Loss of contact caused by short center incisors in an otherwise correct bite shall not be judged undershot.

MAS: A full complement of teeth meet in a scissor bite. Teeth broken, missing or discoloured by accident are not penalized.

DISQUALIFICATION: Undershot or overshot bite.

KIEFER UND ZÄHNE

AUSSIES: Komplettes Scherengebiss mit kräftigen weißen Zähnen; Zangengebiss wird toleriert.

DISQUALIFIKATION: Vorbiß. Rückbiß mit mehr als ⅛ inch (2.5 mm). Kontaktverlust durch kurze zentrale Schneidezähne bei sonst korrektem Gebiss soll nicht als Vorbiß beurteilt werden; abgebrochene oder durch Unfall fehlende Zähne sollen nicht bestraft werden.

MAS: Lückenloses Scherengebiss. Kein Punktabzug bei abgebrochenen, fehlenden oder verfärbten Zähnen infolge von Unfall.

DISQUALIFIKATION: Vorbiß oder Rückbiß.

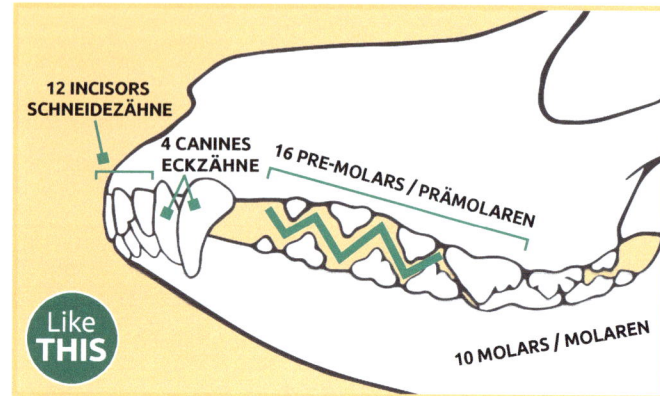

SCISSORS IS IDEAL / So: Schere
Pre-molars and molars align in an even zig-zag pattern. Prämolaren und Molaren sind in einem gleichmäßigen Zickzackmuster angeordnet.

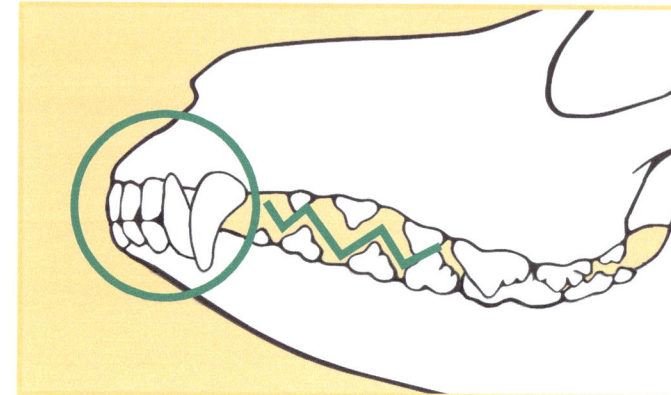

LEVEL or PINCER / So: Zange
Incisors meet at tips. / Die Schneidezähne treffen sich an den Spitzen.
Pre-molars and molars align in a slightly uneven zig-zag pattern. Prämolaren und Molaren sind in einem leicht ungleichmäßigen Zick-Zack-Muster angeordnet.
AUSSIES: Acceptable. MAS: Deviation from ideal.
AUSSIES: Annehmbar. MAS: Abweichung vom Ideal.

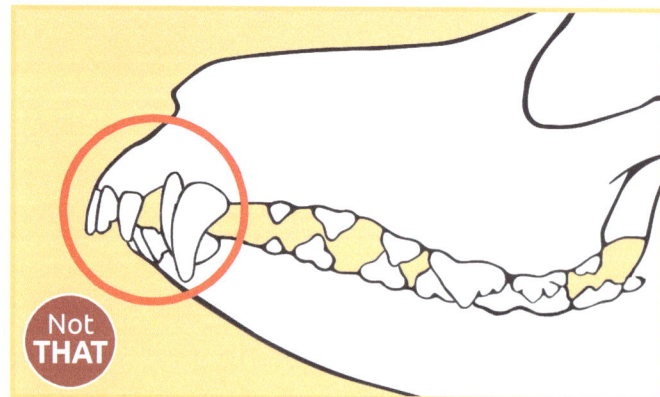

OVERSHOT or OVERBITE / Nicht das: Rückbiss
Upper jaw is longer than lower jaw. Der Oberkiefer ist länger als der Unterkiefer.
Upper incisors protrude beyond lower incisors. / Die oberen Schneidezähne ragen über die unteren Schneidezähne hinaus.
Canine teeth overlap too much. / Die Eckzähne überlappen zu stark.
Pre-molars and molars interfere with each other. Prämolaren und Molaren überschneiden sich.

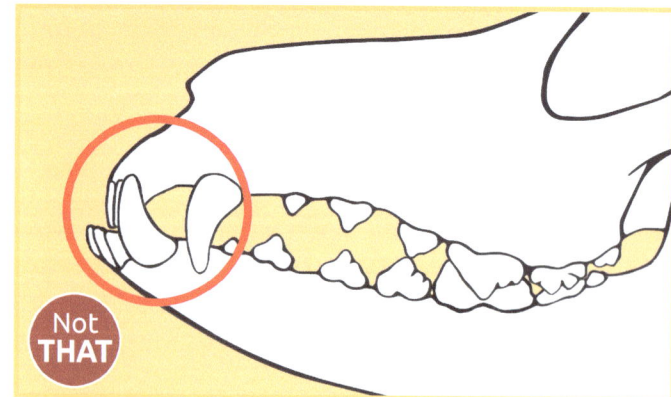

UNDERSHOT or UNDERBITE / Nicht das: Vorbiß
Lower jaw is longer than upper jaw. Der Unterkiefer ist länger als der Oberkiefer.
Lower incisors protrude beyond upper incisors. Untere Schneidezähne ragen über die oberen Schneidezähne hinaus.
Gap between canine teeth. / Lücke zwischen den Eckzähnen (Pfeil).
Pre-molars and molars interfere with each other. Prämolaren und Molaren behindern sich gegenseitig.

PAULA WATERMAN/INKWELL STUDIO PHOTO

ANNE FRANÇOISE PHOTOGRAPHY

Wie das

AUSSIES: The blue merles and blacks have black pigmentation on eye rims. The red merles and reds have liver (brown) pigmentation on eye rims. Nose: Blue merles and blacks have black pigmentation on the nose (and lips). Red merles and reds have liver (brown) pigmentation on the nose (and lips).

Wie das

MAS: The eye rims of the reds and red merles have full red (liver) pigmentation. The eye rims of the blacks and blue merles have full black pigmentation. Nose: Red merles and reds have red (liver) pigmentation on the nose leather. Blue merles and blacks have black pigmentation on the nose leather. Fully pigmented noses are preferred. Lips: Pigment to match colour of dog.

PIGMENTIERUNG VON NASE, AUGENRÄNDERN, LIPPEN

AUSSIES: Die Bluemerle und die Hunde mit schwarzem Haarkleid weisen eine schwarze Augenumrandung auf; die Redmerle und die Hunde mit rotem Haarkleid zeigen eine leberfarbene (braune) Pigmentierung. Nasenschwamm: Bei Bluemerle und bei Hunden mit schwarzem Haarkleid sind der Naschwamm und die Lippen schwarz pigmentiert, bei Redmerle und Hunden mit rotem Haarkleid leberfarben (braun).

MAS: Die Augenränder von roten und rotmelierten Tieren haben eine vollständige rote (leberbraune) Pigmentierung. Die Augenränder der schwarzen und blaumelierten Tiere weisen eine vollständige schwarze Pigmentierung auf. Rot Merle- und rote Hunde haben einen leberfarbenen Nasenspiegel Blau Merle- und schwarze Hunde haben ein schwarzes Nasenpigment. Voll pigmentierte Nasenschwämme werden bevorzugt. Lefzen: Pigmentierung passend zur Farbe des Hundes, enganliegend.

AUSSIES: On merles it is permissible to have small pink spots.

> **SERIOUS FAULT:** More than 25% unpigmented nose leather on dogs over one year of age. No disqualification.

MAS: Fully pigmented noses are preferred. Noses that are less than fully pigmented will be faulted.

> **SEVERE FAULT:** 25 to 50% unpigmented nose leather.
> **DISQUALIFICATION:** More than 50% unpigmented nose leather.

WHY?
Pink noses are at higher risk for sun damage which can potentially become cancerous. This is highly undesirable for dogs who spend a significant amount of time outdoors.

NASENPIGMENTIERUNG

AUSSIES: Bei den merlefarbenen Hunden sind kleine rosarote Flecken zulässig.

> **GRAVIERENDER FEHLER:** Mehr als 25% unpigmentierter Nasenschwamm bei Hunden über ein Jahr alt. Keine Disqualifikation.

MAS: Voll pigmentierte Nasenschwamm werden bevorzugt. Nasenschwamm, die nicht vollständig pigmentiert sind, sind ein Fehler.

> **SCHWERER FEHLER:** Zwischen 25 und 50% unpigmentierter Nasenschwamm.
> **DISQUALIFIKATION:** Mehr als 50% fehlende Pigmentierung am Nasenschwamm.

WARUM?
Rosa Nasen haben ein höheres Risiko für Sonnenschädigungen, die möglicherweise krebserregend sein können. Dies ist für Hunde, die viel Zeit im Freien verbringen, höchst unerwünscht.

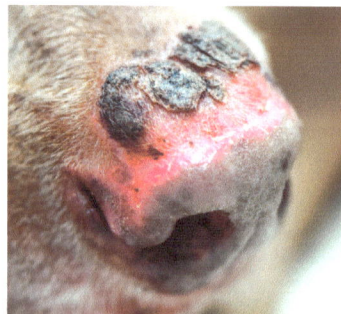

Sun damage / Sonnenschädigungen

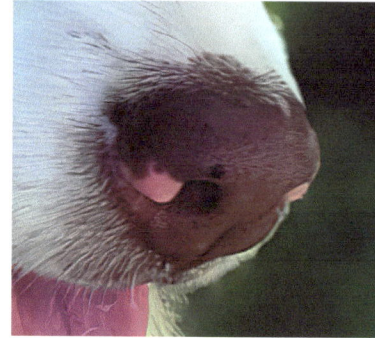

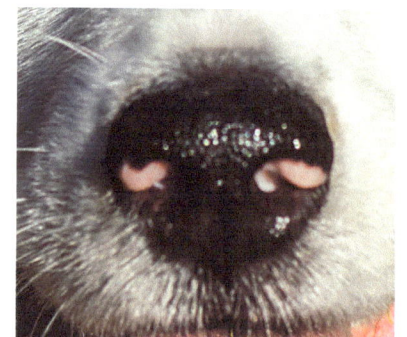

LESS THAN 25% UNPIGMENTED NOSE
WENIGER ALS 25% UNPIGMENTIERTE NASENSCHWAMM

AUSSIES: On merles it is permissible to have small pink spots. / Bei den merlefarbenen Hunden sind kleine rosarote Flecken zulässig.

MAS: FAULT. Fully pigmented noses are preferred. Noses that are less than fully pigmented will be faulted.
/ **FEHLER.** Voll pigmentierte Nasenschwamm werden bevorzugt. Nasenschwamm, die nicht vollständig pigmentiert sind, sind ein Fehler.

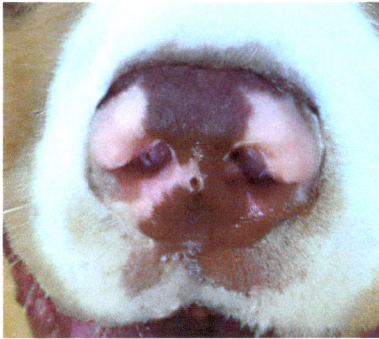

25% TO 50% UNPIGMENTED NOSE LEATHER
ZWISCHEN 25 UND 50% UNPIGMENTIERTER NASENSCHWAMM

AUSSIES: SERIOUS FAULT. More than 25% unpigmented nose leather on dogs over one year of age. / **GRAVIERENDER FEHLER.** Mehr als 25% unpigmentierter Nasenschwamm bei Hunden über ein Jahr alt.

MAS: SEVERE FAULT. 25 to 50% unpigmented nose leather. / **SCHWERER FEHLER.** Zwischen 25 und 50% unpigmentierter Nasenschwamm.

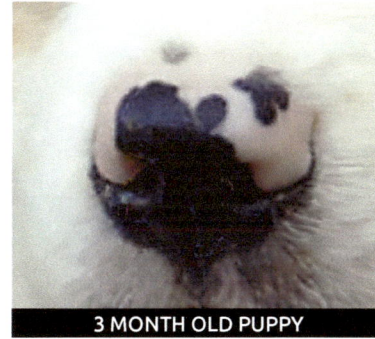

3 MONTH OLD PUPPY
3 MONATE ALTER WELPEN

PUPPY'S NOSE FILLED IN BY 2 YRS
WELPENNASE UM 2 JAHRE GEFÜLLT

Noses often fill in with pigment as dogs mature.

Die Nasen füllen sich oft mit Pigment, wenn die Hunde älter werden.

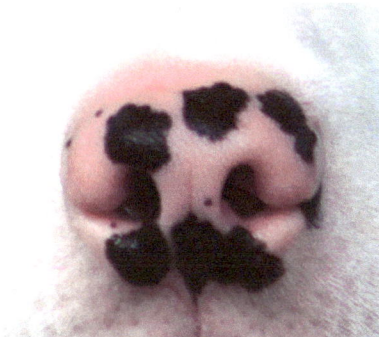

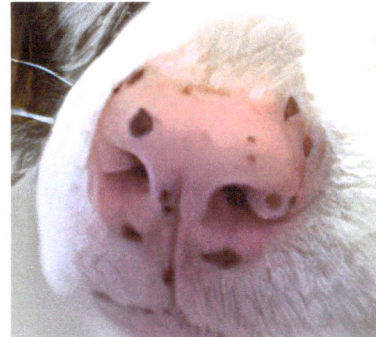

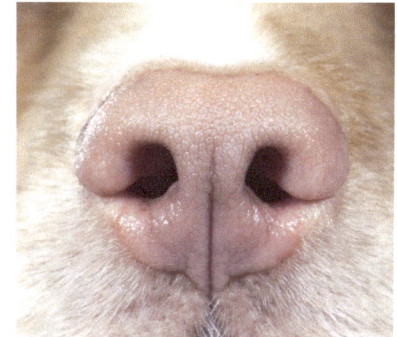

MORE THAN 50% UNPIGMENTED NOSE LEATHER / MEHR ALS 50% UNPIGMENTIERTER NASENSCHWAMM

AUSSIES: SERIOUS FAULT. More than 25% unpigmented nose leather on dogs over one year of age. No disqualification. / **GRAVIERENDER FEHLER.** Mehr als 25% unpigmentierter Nasenschwamm bei Hunden über ein Jahr alt. Keine Disqualifikation.

MAS: DISQUALIFICATION. More than 50% unpigmented nose leather. / **DISQUALIFIKATION.** Mehr als 50% fehlende Pigmentierung am Nasenschwamm.

PAULA MCDERMID PHOTO

Eyes, Ears, Expression

Augen, Ausdruck, Ohren

Like THIS

Alle diese Augen sind richtig

Eye colour

One or both eyes may be brown, blue, hazel, amber or any colour combination thereof, including flecks and marbling. Acceptable in all coat colours.

Eye shape

AUSSIES: Almond shaped, not protruding nor sunken.

MAS: The eyes are set obliquely, almond shaped, neither protruding nor sunken and in proportion to the head.

AUGENFORM UND -FARBE

Augenfarbe

Akzeptabel in allen Fellfarben kann ein oder beide Augen braun, blau, haselnussbraun, bernsteinfarben oder jede Farbkombination aufweisen, einschließlich Tüpfel und Marmorierung.

Augenform

AUSSIES: Mandelförmig, weder vorstehend noch eingesunken.

MAS: Die Augen sind schräg angesetzt, mandelförmig, weder hervorstehend noch eingesunken und proportional zum Kopf.

PAULA MCDERMID PHOTO

PAULA MCDERMID PHOTO

MICHAEL TWESTEN PHOTOGRAPHY

PENNY BROOKS, PENZ PHOTOZ

Like
THIS

Blue eyes are correct and equally desirable in ALL coat colours including blue merle, black, red merle, and red.

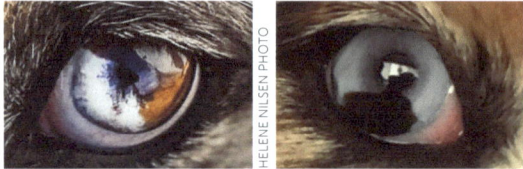

HELENE NILSEN PHOTO

MARY ARNOLD PHOTO

Marbled eyes / Marmorierte Augen

Marbled eyes. In merles, eyes can be marbled with flecks and blotches of brown, amber, or blue. Marbling occurs in the iris (the coloured area in the eye). The pupil (the black center of the eye) is perfectly round. Marbling should not be confused with iris coloboma, which is a defect that may look like an irregularly-shaped pupil or a notch or hole in the iris.

AUGENFARBE

Blaue Augen sind in allen Fellfarben richtig und gleichermaßen wünschenswert, siehe Abbildung blaue Augen bei Blue Merle, Black, Red Merle und Red.

Marmorierte Augen. Bei Merles können die Augen mit braunen, bernsteinfarbenen oder blauen Flecken marmoriert sein. Die Marmorierung befindet sich in der Iris (dem farbigen Bereich des Auges). Die Pupille (die schwarze Mitte des Auges) ist vollkommen rund. Die Marmorierung ist nicht zu verwechseln mit dem Iris-Kolobom, einem Defekt, der wie eine unregelmäßig geformte Pupille oder eine Kerbe oder ein Loch in der Iris aussehen kann.

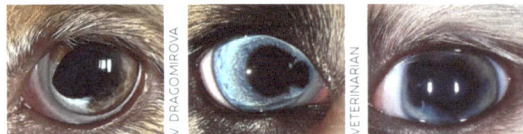

V DRAGOMIROVA

VETERINARIAN

C PELTIER

Iris coloboma / Iris-Kolobom

INGA CERBULE PHOTO

TATRANSKÁ LABKA

NADIA SOPHIE VON SCHLAPP PHOTO

HAYLEY LAMB PHOTO

Not THAT

Alle diese Augen sind fehlerhaft

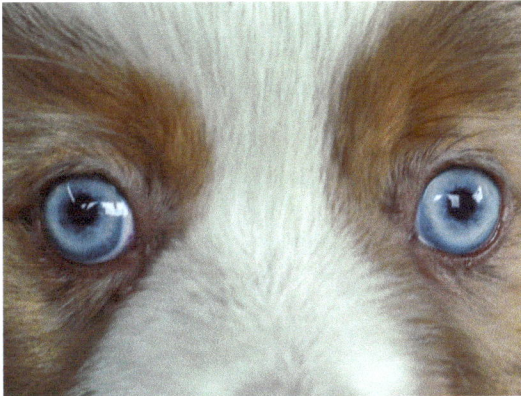

Round eyes / Runde Augen

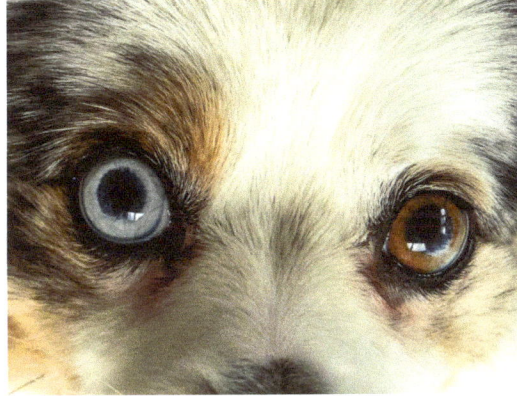

Protruding eyes / Hervorstehende Augen

Drooping lower eyelids (haws or ectropion)
Hängende Unterlider (Haws/ Ektropium)

Eyes should be almond-shaped

Eye shape faults are caused by incorrect head structure resulting in poorly-positioned eyes and eye sockets.

Drooping lower eyelids (haws or ectropion) can be caused by loose skin on the head or weak lower eyelid muscles.

- Eyes should not be round, neither protruding nor sunken.
- Eye rims should be tight and whites of eyes should not be visible.

WHY?

- Protruding eyes are vulnerable to injury from debris and physical trauma.
- Drooping lower eyelids (haws/ectropion) expose the delicate tissue of the inner eyelid, which can result in painful corneal inflammation, corneal scarring, and impaired vision. Haws can trap seeds, dirt, and debris that can injure the eyes.
- Eyes with drooping lower eyelids (haws/ectropion), and round or bulging eyes detract from correct expression.

AUGENFORM

Augen sollten mandelförmig sein

Fehler in der Augenform werden durch eine falsche Kopfanatomie verursacht, die zu schlecht positionierten Augen und Augenhöhlen führt.

Hängende Unterlider (Haws/ Ektropium) können durch lose Haut am Kopf oder schwache Unterlidmuskeln verursacht werden.

- Die Augen sollten nicht rund sein, weder hervorstehend noch eingefallen.
- Die Augenränder sollten eng anliegen und das Weiß der Augen sollte nicht sichtbar sein.

WARUM?

- Hervortretende Augen sind anfällig für Verletzungen durch Trümmerteile und physische Traumata.
- Hängende Unterlider (Haws/ Ektropium) legen das empfindliche innere Augenlidgewebe frei, was zu schmerzhaften Hornhautentzündungen, Hornhautvernarbungen und Sehstörungen führen kann. Haws können Samen, Schmutz und Ablagerungen einschließen, die die Augen verletzen können.
- Augen mit hängenden Unterlidern (Haws/ Ektropium), runden oder vorgewölbten Augen stören den korrekten Ausdruck.

Diese Ohren sind richtig

Ear size and shape

Ears should be triangular, of moderate size and leather, set high on the head. At full attention the ears break forward and over, or to the side as a rose ear.

One ear can break to the side and the other ear can break forward.

What is moderate ear size?

When pulled gently forward, the tip of the ear should reach the inside corner of the nearest eye.

OHREN

Dreieckig, von mäßiger Größe und Dicke, hoch am Kopf angesetzt. Bei voller Aufmerksamkeit kippen die Ohren nach vorne oder nach der Seite wie ein Rosenohr.

Dabei kann die Ohrhaltung auch unterschiedlich sein: ein Ohr bricht zur Seite, das andere nach vorne.

Was ist eine mäßige Ohrgröße?

Wenn man das Ohr leicht nach vorne zieht, sollte die Ohrspitze den inneren Augenwinkel erreichen.

DIRK BOSSELMANN PHOTO

SHIELA POLK TRIHVORY

PAULA MCDERMID PHOTO

PAULA MCDERMID PHOTO

Like THIS

Das ist der richtige Ausdruck

AUSSIES: Showing attentiveness and intelligence, alert and eager. Gaze should be keen but friendly.

MAS: Alert, attentive, and intelligent. They may express a reserved look or be watchful of strangers.

AUSDRUCK

AUSSIES: Aufmerksam und intelligent, wachsam und lebhaft. Der Blick ist durchdringend, aber freundlich.

MAS: Aufgeweckt, aufmerksam und intelligent. Der Blick kann Fremden gegenüber reserviert oder aufmerksam sein.

MELISSA ZOBELL BREEDER · PHOTOGRAPHER

ISABELLE GUILLOT PHOTOGRAPHY

SOUTH RAM OUFITTERS PHOTO

SOPHIE TROTIER PHOTO

TATRANSKÁ LABKA

Not THAT

Diese Ohren sind nicht richtig

Ears too large. Dotted yellow lines show size the ears should be. / **Ohren zu groß.** Die gestrichelten gelben Linien zeigen die Größe der Ohren an.

Hanging hound ears / Hängeohren

Prick ears / Stehohren

Hanging ears: SEVERE FAULT

WHY?

- Excess ear leather has greater risk of being torn; ears are more susceptible to infections.
- Large pendulous ears give an uncharacteristic droopy expression.

Aussie expression: Showing attentiveness and intelligence, alert and eager. Gaze should be keen but friendly.

MAS expression: Alert, attentive, and intelligent. They may express a reserved look or be watchful of strangers.

Prick ears: SEVERE FAULT

WHY?

- They detract from correct breed character.

Prick and hound-type ears are **SEVERELY FAULTED** for detracting significantly from breed character, but are not disqualified because of the relative unimportance of earset compared to structural soundness.

OHRFEHLER

Hängeohre: SCHWERER FEHLER

WARUM?

- Überschüssiges Ohrleder hat ein größeres Risiko, dass es reißt; Ohren sind anfälliger für Infektionen.
- Große hängende Ohren geben einen uncharakteristischen schlaffen Ausdruck.

Aussie-Ausdruck: Aufmerksam und intelligent, wachsam und lebhaft. Der Blick ist durchdringend, aber freundlich.

MAS-Ausdruck: Der Ausdruck ist aufgeweckt, aufmerksam und intelligent. Der Blick kann Fremden gegenüber reserviert oder aufmerksam sein.

Stehohren: SCHWERER FEHLER

WARUM?

- Sie den Rassecharakter erheblich beeinträchtigen.

Stehohren oder Hängeohren sind **SCHWERE FEHLER**, da sie den Rassecharakter erheblich beeinträchtigen, werden jedoch wegen der relativen Bedeutungslosigkeit des Ohransatzes im Vergleich zur strukturellen Gesundheit nicht als disqualifizierender Fehler aufgeführt.

KERRY SPARKS / DALLY UP PHOTOGRAPHY

Body
Moderate and Athletic

Körper
Moderat und Athletisch

Like THIS
Wie das

Males reflect masculinity without coarseness.

RÜDEN

Der Körperbau des Rüden ist geschlechtstypisch kräftig,
ohne jedoch derb zu wirken.

Like
THIS

Wie das

Bitches appear feminine without being slight of bone.

HÜNDIN

Die Hündin ist sehr weiblich in ihrem Aussehen, jedoch ohne
jegliche Schwäche in ihrem Knochenbau.

Neck

Strong, of moderate length, slightly arched at the crest, fitting well into the shoulders.

Chest

Not broad, but deep with the lowest point reaching the elbow.

Ribs

Well sprung and long, neither barrel chested nor slab-sided.

AUSSIES:

The width of the hindquarters is *equal to* the width of the forequarters at the shoulder.

MAS:

Width of hindquarters is *approximately equal to* the width of the forequarters at the shoulders.

KÖRPER

Hals

Der Hals ist fest, sauber und proportional zum Körper. Er ist von mittlerer Länge und am Kamm leicht gebogen, mit gutem Übergang zur Schulterpartie.

Brust

Nicht breit, dafür aber tief: sie reicht an ihrem tiefsten Punkt bis zur Höhe der Ellenbogen.

Rippen

Lang und gut gewölbt; der Brustkorb ist weder tonnenförmig noch flach.

Die Breite der Hinterhand erreicht ungefähr die Breite der Vorderhand an den Schultern.

Wie das

Wie das

Topline

Back straight and strong, level and firm from withers to hip joints when standing or moving.

WHY?

A strong, level topline enables efficient trotting at consistent speeds for long periods of time.

Croup

Moderately sloping.

Underline

Shows a moderate tuck-up.

OBERLINIE UND KRUPPE

Oberlinie

Der Rücken ist im Stand und in der Bewegung vom Widerrist zu den Hüften fest und gerade.

WARUM?

Eine starke, ebene Oberlinie ermöglicht effizientes Traben bei konstanter Geschwindigkeit über lange Zeiträume.

Kruppe

Mäßig abfallend.

Untere Profillinie

Mäßig aufgezogen.

Like THIS

Wie das

Not THAT

Nicht das

AUSSIES:

- Shoulder-blades: long, flat, fairly close set at the withers and well laid back.

- Upper arm: should be relatively the same length as the shoulder-blade, attaches at an approximate right angle to the shoulder line with forelegs dropping straight, perpendicular to the ground.

MAS:

- Shoulder blades (scapula) are long, flat, fairly close set at the withers, and well laid back.

- The upper arm (humerus) is equal in length to the shoulder blade and meets the shoulder blade at an approximate right angle.

- The elbow joint is equidistant from the ground to the withers. Viewed from the side, the elbow should be directly under the withers. The elbows should be close to the ribs without looseness.

VORDERHAND

AUSSIES:

- Schulterblätter: Lang, flach und gut schräg gelagert; Schulterblattkuppen am Widerrist ziemlich nahe beieinanderliegend.

- Oberarm: Sollte ungefähr gleich lang sein wie das Schulterblatt; er steht ungefähr in einem rechten Winkel zum Schulterblatt, mit geraden und senkrecht zu Boden stehenden Vorderläufen.

MAS:

- Schulterblätter: Lang, flach, eng am Widerrist angesetzt und schräg.

- Oberarm: Die Länge des Oberarms (Oberarmknochen) ist mit der des Schulterblatts identisch und steht in einem nahezu rechten Winkel zum Schulterblatt.

- Ellbogen: Das Ellbogengelenk ist vom Boden bis zum Widerrist abstandsgleich. Von der Seite gesehen sollte der Ellbogen direkt unter dem Widerrist sitzen. Ellbogen sollen eng an den Rippen anliegen, ohne locker zu sein.

Wie das

Nicht das

Balance

The angulation of the pelvis and upper thigh corresponds to the angulation of the shoulder-blade and upper arm, forming an approximate right angle.

WHY?

When the front and rear angulation correspond, the dog is in balance. The thrust of the rear quarters is transmitted to the forequarters smoothly and with no loss of power.

More is not better

Correct angulation is the amount that enables a dog to do the job for which it was originally bred. Both too little and too much angulation reduce endurance.

AUSGEWOGENE WINKELUNG

Balance

Die Winkelung von Becken und Oberschenkel (Oberschenkelknochen) spiegelt die Winkelung von Schulterblatt und Oberarm wider; es wird ungefähr ein rechter Winkel gebildet.

WARUM?

Wenn die vordere und hintere Winkelung übereinstimmen, ist der Hund im Gleichgewicht. Der Schub der Hinterhand wird sanft und ohne Kraftverlust auf die Vorderhand übertragen.

Mehr ist nicht besser

Die korrekt Winkelung ist die Winkelung, die es einem Hund ermöglicht, die Arbeit zu erledigen, für die er ursprünglich gezüchtet wurde. Sowohl zu wenig als auch zu viel Winkelung verringern die Ausdauer.

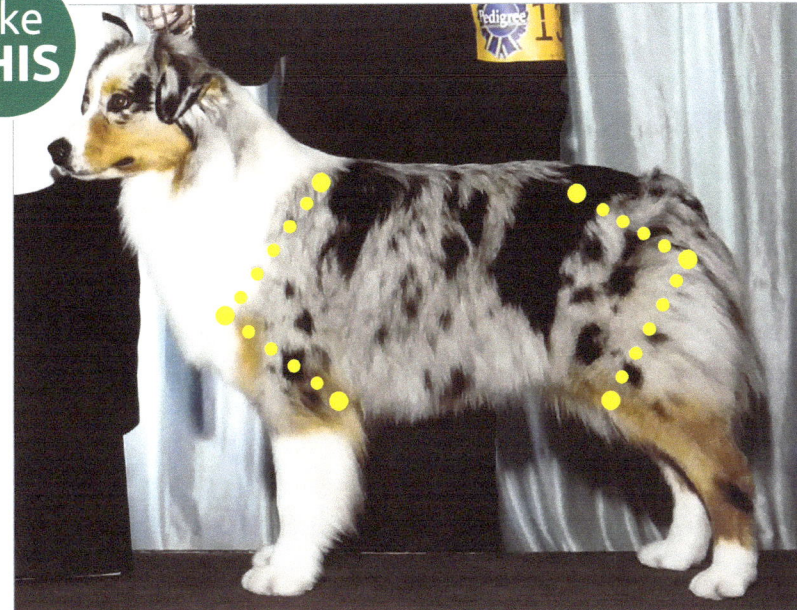

Wie das

Nicht das

Like **THIS**

Wie das

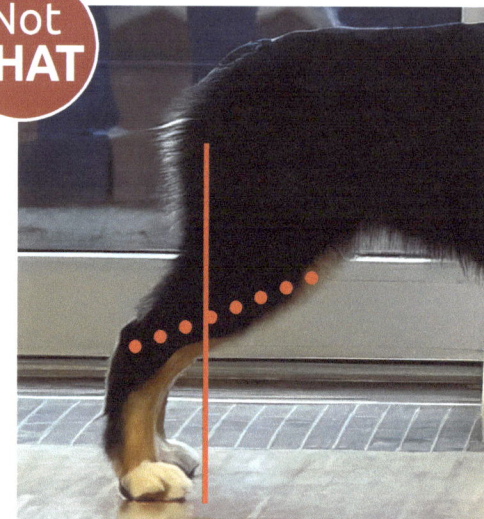

Not **THAT**

Nicht das

MARCO ROSETTI PHOTOGRAPHY

Stifle: Clearly defined.

Hock joints: *Moderately* bent.

Hocks: Short, perpendicular to the ground and parallel to each other when viewed from the rear.

Knie: Klar definiert.

Sprunggelenke: *Mäßig* gebogen.

Sprunggelenke: Kurz, senkrecht zum Boden und von hinten gesehen parallel zueinander.

CORRECT: This dog has **moderate** angulation of the hindquarters and correct length of bones between knee and hock joints, *as shown by the dotted yellow line.* When viewed from the side, with the hocks forming a right angle to the ground, the correct angles and correct length of bones place his rear feet directly underneath the bones he sits on, *as shown by the solid yellow line.* This structure provides greater accuracy of rear foot placement and gives the best combination of speed, endurance, and maneuverability. This dog is able to accelerate rapidly, stop instantly, and change direction and gait quickly.

INCORRECT: This dog has **excess** angulation of the hindquarters, and the bones between his knee and hock joints are too long, *as shown by the dotted red line.* When viewed from the side, with the hocks forming a right angle to the ground, the excess angles and excess length of bones cause his rear feet to be placed far out behind the bones he sits on, *as shown by the solid red line.* This structure enables a longer trotting stride but reduces stamina, stability, and the ability to stop quickly and turn sharply. It requires greater muscular strength and coordination to stabilize the hindquarters. Any potential advantage in trotting ability is offset by muscular instability.

HINTERHAND

Korrekt: Dieser Hund hat eine morderate Winkelung der Hinterhand und eine korrekte Länge der Knochen zwischen Knie- und Sprunggelenken, wie durch die gestrichelte gelbe Linie dargestellt. Von der Seite gesehen, wenn die Sprunggelenke einen rechten Winkel zum Boden bilden, platzieren die korrekten Winkel und die korrekte Länge der Knochen seine Hinterpfoten direkt unter dem Sitzbeinhöcker, wie durch die durchgezogene gelbe Linie dargestellt. Diese Struktur ermöglicht eine genauere Platzierung der Hinterpfoten und bietet die beste Kombination aus Schnelligkeit, Ausdauer und Manövrierfähigkeit. Dieser Hund ist in der Lage, schnell zu beschleunigen, sofort anzuhalten und die Richtung und die Gangart schnell zu ändern.

Falsch: Bei diesem Hund ist die Hinterhand zu stark gewinkelt, und die Knochen zwischen Knie- und Sprunggelenk sind zu lang, wie die gestrichelte rote Linie zeigt. Von der Seite gesehen, wenn die Sprunggelenke einen rechten Winkel zum Boden bilden, führen die übermäßigen Winkel und die übermäßige Länge der Knochen dazu, dass die Hinterpfoten weit hinter dem Sitzbeinhöcker platziert sind, wie die durchgezogene rote Linie zeigt. Diese Struktur ermöglicht einen längeren Trabschritt, verringert jedoch die Ausdauer, die Stabilität und die Fähigkeit, schnell anzuhalten und scharf abzubiegen. Die Stabilisierung der Hinterhand erfordert mehr Muskelkraft und Koordination. Jeder potenzielle Vorteil bei der Trabfähigkeit wird durch die muskuläre Instabilität wieder aufgehoben.

Legs: Straight and strong. Bone strong, oval rather than round.

Feet: Oval, compact, with close-knit, well-arched toes. Pads thick and resilient.

Front Metacarpus (pastern):

AUSSIES: Medium length, very slightly sloping.
MAS: Short, thick and strong, but still flexible, showing a slight angle when viewed from the side.

Dewclaws:

AUSSIES: Front dewclaws may be removed.*
MAS: Dewclaws should be removed.*
* except where forbidden by law

REAR DEWCLAW
Hintere Afterkralle

JULIA BETTENDORF PHOTOGRAPHY

Rear Metatarsus (rear pastern/hock): Short, perpendicular to the ground and parallel to each other when viewed from the rear.

AUSSIES: No rear dewclaws.
MAS: Rear dewclaws should be removed (in countries where it is not forbidden by law).

LÄUFE UND PFOTEN

Läufe: Gerade und stark. Der Knochen ist eher oval als rund.

Pfoten: Oval, kompakt, mit eng an einander liegenden, gut gewölbten Zehen. Ballen dick und elastisch.

MAS: Die Nägel sind kurz und stark und können jede Farbkombination aufweisen.

Vordermittelfuß:

AUSSIES: Von mittlerer Länge, sehr leicht schräg.
MAS: Kurz, dick und stark, jedoch flexibel, von der Seite gesehen in einem leichten Winkel stehend.

Afterkrallen:

AUSSIES: Afterkrallen können entfernt werden.*
MAS: Afterkrallen müssen entfernt werden*
* (in Ländern, in welchen dies gesetzlich nicht verboten ist).

Hintermittelfuß: Kurz, von der Seite gesehen lotrecht zum Boden und sie stehen von hinten gesehen parallel zueinander.

AUSSIES: Afterkrallen müssen entfernt sein.

Aussies and MAS must have sound feet to accomplish their tasks.

Aussies und MAS müssen gesunde Füße haben, um ihre Aufgaben erfüllen zu können.

AUSSIE FRONT FEET & PASTERNS

ELISABETH EKNES PHOTOGRAPHY

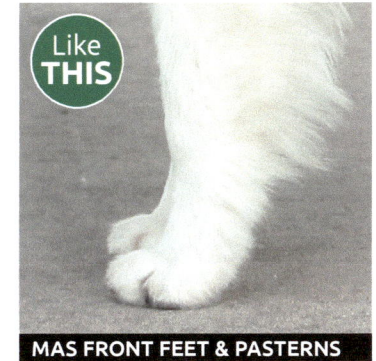

MAS FRONT FEET & PASTERNS

DAVE BIRREN PHOTO

DEFINITION: Oval feet. The two center toes are slightly longer than the outer and inner toes./ **Ovale Füße.** Die beiden mittleren Zehen sind etwas länger als die äußeren und inneren Zehen.

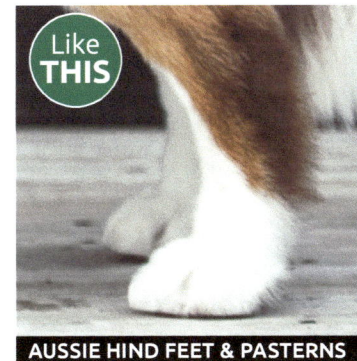

AUSSIE HIND FEET & PASTERNS

ELISABETH EKNES PHOTOGRAPHY

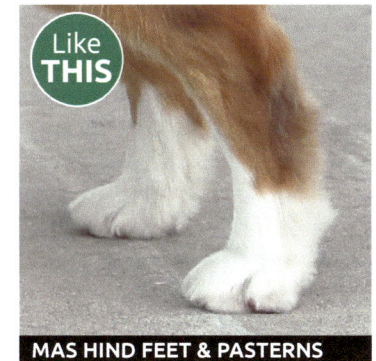

MAS HIND FEET & PASTERNS

DAVE BIRREN PHOTO

Oben: Aussie Vorderpfoten und Vordermittelfuß. Unten: Aussie Hinterpfoten und Hintermittelfuß

Oben: MAS Vorderpfoten und Vordermittelfuß. Unten: MAS Hinterpfoten und Hintermittelfuß

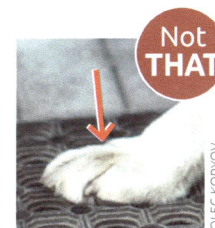

OLEG KOPYOV

FEHLER **Nicht das: Flat feet** / Senkfüß

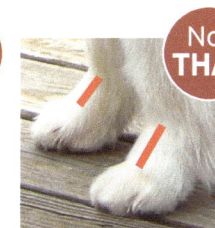

PAULA MCDERMID

FEHLER **Nicht das: Weak pasterns** / Schwacher Vordermittelfuß

KIMBERLY DAEMERS

FEHLER **Nicht das: Toe pads tip upward** / Die Zehenpolster kippen nach oben

Diese sind korrekt, mit Ausnahme der geringelten Rute, die unten rechts

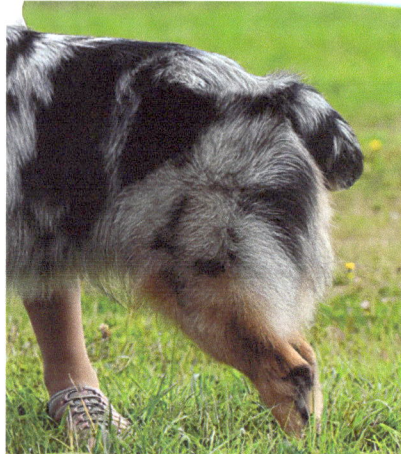

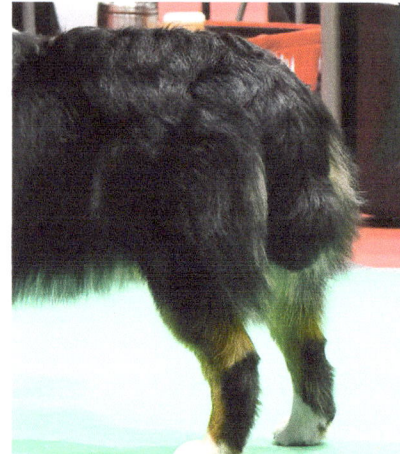

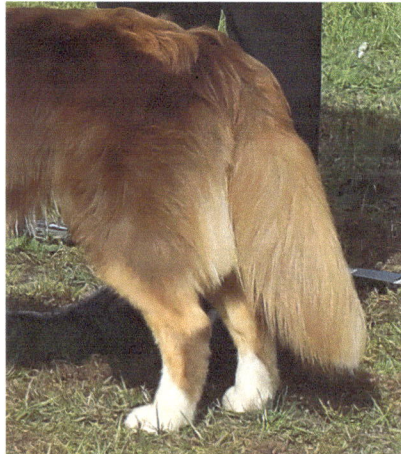

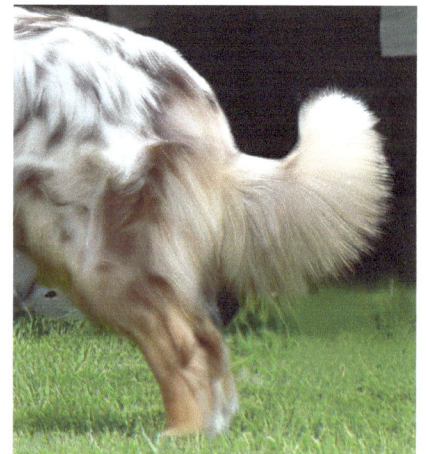

AUSSIES: In countries where docking is allowed, the tail should not exceed 10 cm (4 inches). Where docking is not allowed, the tail can be any length with no preference.

MAS: A docked or natural bobtail is preferred. A docked tail is straight, not to exceed exceed 7.5 cm (3 inches) in countries where it is not forbidden by law.

RUTE IM STAND

AUSSIES: In Ländern in welchen kupieren erlaubt ist, sollte die Rute nicht länger als 10 cm (4 inches) sein. Wo kupieren nicht erlaubt ist, kann die Länger der Rute ohne Präferenz variieren.

MAS: Eine kupierte oder natürliche Stummelrute wird bevorzugt. Die kupierte Rute ist gerade, nicht länger als 7,5 cm (3 Zoll) in Ländern, in welchen dies gesetzlich nicht verboten ist. Die nicht kupierte Rute kann in einer leichten Rundung herabhängen, wenn der Hund ruht.

Das sind alle richtig

MAS: The undocked tail when at rest may hang in a slight curve. When excited or in motion the tail may be carried raised with the curve accentuated.

AUSSIES: Standard does not address tail carriage.

RUTE IN BEWEGUNG

MAS: Die nicht kupierte Rute kann in einer leichten Rundung herabhängen, wenn der Hund ruht. Bei Erregung oder in der Bewegung kann die Rute in einer ausgeprägten Rundung nach oben getragen werden.

AUSSIES: Bezieht sich nicht auf die Rutenhaltung.

MONIQUE GAUTREAUX PHOTOGRAPHY

Movement
Balanced and Effortless

Bewegung
Ausbalanciert und Mühelos

Efficient movement is effortless with feet moving close to the ground.

Effiziente Bewegung ist mühelos: die Füße bewegen sich nah am Boden und so wird keine unnötige Energie verschwendet wird.

Smooth, free and easy gait.

Great agility of movement with a well-balanced, ground covering stride.

AUSSIES: Animated, lithe and agile.

MAS: Exceptional agility combined with strength and stamina allows for working over a variety of terrain.

GANGWERK

Geschmeidig, leicht und frei.

Der Gang ist fließend, frei, leicht und geschmeidig , mit einem gut ausgewogenen, raumgreifenden Schritt. Er ist sehr behände mit einem harmonischen, raumgreifenden Bewegungsablauf.

Er muss flink und fähig sein, augenblicklich einen Richtungswechsel vorzunehmen oder ein andere Gangart einzuschlagen.

Not
THAT

Nicht das

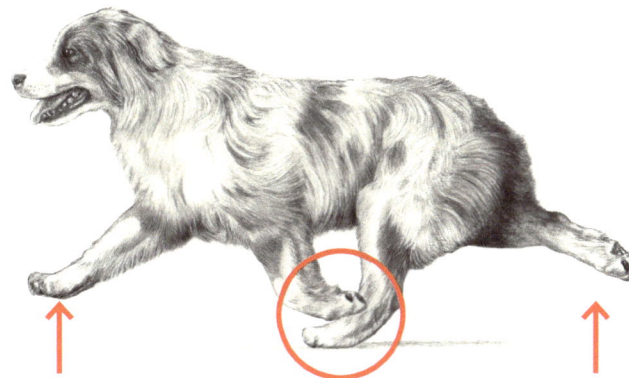

Legs lift high off the ground and interfere with each other under the dog. This wastes energy and prevents the dog from being able to work all day. A structurally correct dog can be forced to move incorrectly by trotting him too fast.

Die Läufe sind in der Luft und beeinträchtigen sich gegenseitig, wenn sie unter dem Körper zusammentreffen. Dies verschwendet Energie und verhindert, dass der Hund den ganzen Tag arbeiten kann. Ein strukturell korrekter Hund kann durch zu schnelles Traben zu falschen Bewegungen gezwungen werden.

Like **THIS**

Wie das

MICHAEL ENGLISH PHOTOGRAPHY

GUNTER NAFFIEN PHOTO

AUSSIES: The gait is smooth, free and easy. He exhibits great agility of movement with a well-balanced, ground-covering stride.

MAS: The gait is smooth, free and easy, exhibiting agility of movement with a well-balanced, ground-covering stride. When traveling at a trot, the head is carried in a natural position with the neck extended forward and head nearly level or slightly above the topline.

SEITENGANG

AUSSIES: Die Gangart des australischen Schäferhundes ist geschmeidig, leicht und frei. Er ist sehr behände mit einem harmonischen, raumgreifenden Bewegungsablauf.

MAS: Der Gang ist fließend, frei, leicht und geschmeidig , mit einem gut ausgewogenen, raumgreifenden Schritt. Im Trab wird der Kopf in seiner natürlichen Position getragen, wobei der Hals sich nach Vorne verlängert und der Kopf nahezu in einer Linie zur Rückenlinie oder geringfügig darüber getragen wird.

KAREN DELONG PHOTOGRAPHY

Like
THIS

Wie das

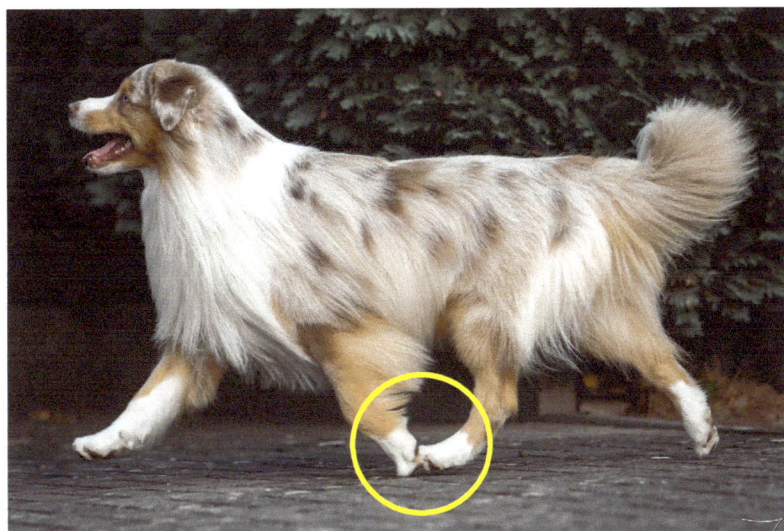

The rear paw lands in the footprint of the front paw.
Feet skim the ground with no excess or wasted motion.

Die Hinterpfote landet im Fußabdruck der Vorderpfote.
Die Füße gleiten über den Boden ohne übermäßige oder
verschwendete Bewegung.

Like THIS

Wie das

HELENE NILSEN PHOTOGRAPHY

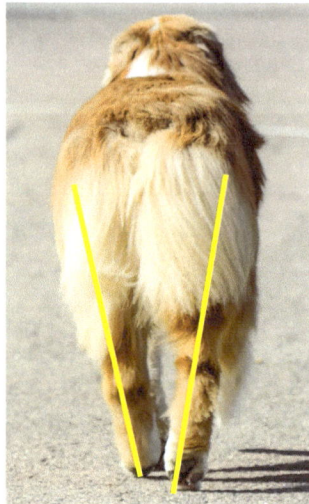

HELENE NILSEN PHOTOGRAPHY

CONNIE DUNCAN PHOTO HART II'S SHORTY BRED BY NORMA HART

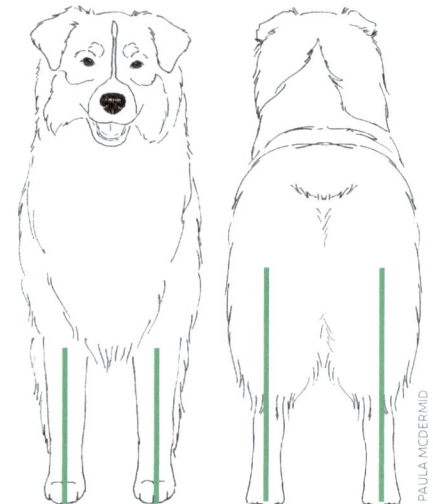

PAULA MCDERMID

Correct Movement

- Legs move in a straight column of support from the shoulders and hips to the feet.
- As speed increases, the feet converge toward the center line of gravity, resembling a "V" shape, in order to maintain side-to-side balance (photos 1 and 2).
- When viewed from the front, as the dog moves, the front leg on one side of the body hides the rear leg on the same side because the dog's spine is straight with the line of travel (photo 1).
- Correct structure enables the dog to move with powerful, efficient reach and drive.

BEWEGUNG DOWN AND BACK

Korrekte Bewegung

- Die Beine bewegen sich in einer geraden Stützsäule von den Schultern und der Hüfte bis zu den Pfoten.
- Mit zunehmender Geschwindigkeit nähern sich die Füße dem Schwerpunkt an und bilden ein "V", um das seitliche Gleichgewicht zu halten (Fotos 1 und 2).
- Von vorne betrachtet, verdeckt das vordere Bein auf einer Seite des Körpers das hintere Bein auf derselben Seite, da die Wirbelsäule des Hundes in gerader Linie verläuft (Foto 1).
- Eine korrekte Struktur ermöglicht es dem Hund, sich mit kraftvollem, effizientem Vortrieb zu bewegen.

Correct Stance

The forelegs drop straight and perpendicular to the ground.

The hocks are short, perpendicular to the ground and parallel to each other when viewed from the rear.

Richtige Haltung

Die Vorderläufe stehen gerade und senkrecht, die Sprunggelenke sind kurz und parallel zueinander, wenn man sie von hinten betrachtet.

The trot reveals the faults and virtues of a dog's conformation. Poor structure diminishes the efficiency and power of the gait and increases stress on the ligaments and tendons that support joints, which can result in pain and injury.

This page shows common movement faults that are evaluated when the dog is trotting away from and towards the judge. Incorrect movement of the legs exposes structural deficiencies of the front and rear assemblies as well as weak tendons and ligaments and unstable joint conformation.

FEHLER IN DER BEWEGUNG

Der Trab offenbart die Fehler und Vorzüge des Körperbaus eines Hundes. Eine schlechte Struktur vermindert die Effizienz und Kraft des Ganges und erhöht die Belastung der Bänder und Sehnen, die Gelenke stützen, was zu Schmerzen und Verletzungen führen kann.

Diese Seite zeigt häufige Bewegungsfehler, die bewertet werden, wenn der Hund im Trab vom Richter weg und auf ihn zu läuft. Eine fehlerhafte Bewegung der Beine offenbart strukturelle Mängel des vorderen und hinteren Aufbaus sowie schwache Sehnen und Bänder und eine instabile Gelenkkonformation.

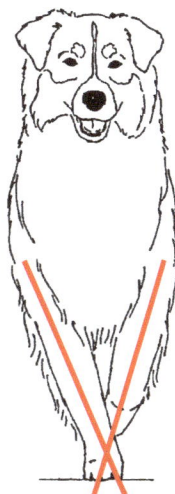

CROSSING OVER
Überkreuzen

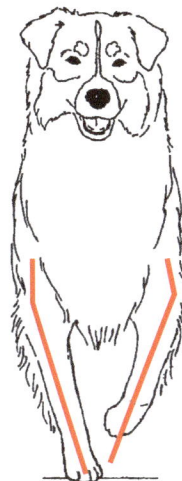

OUT AT ELBOWS
Lose Ellenbogen

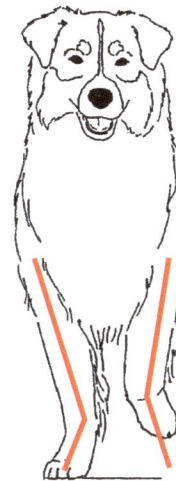

PADDLING
Paddeln

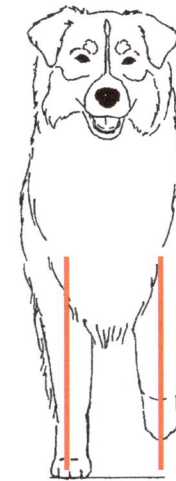

PARALLEL TRACKING
Parallel

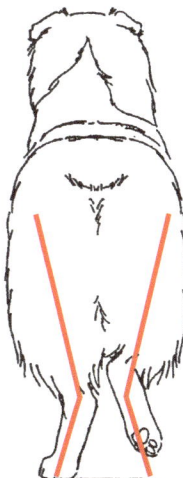

COW HOCKED
Kuhhessig

MOVING CLOSE
Bodeneng

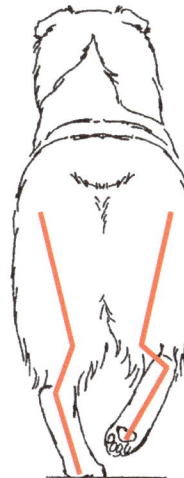

BOWHOCKED
Faßbeinig

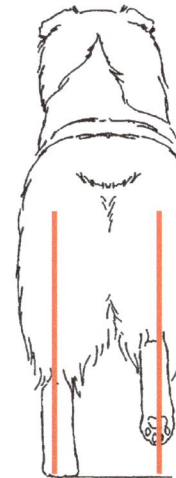

PARALLEL TRACKING
Parallel

PAULA MCDERMID

Free and easy movement of a well-balanced dog.
Freier und leichter Bewegungsablauf eines gut
ausbalancierten Hundes.

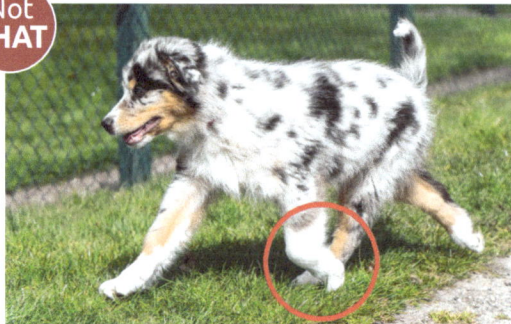

More rear angulation than front angulation
Mehr Hinterhandwinkelung als Vorderhandwinkelung

More front angulation than rear angulation
Mehr Vorderhandwinkelung als Hinterhandwinkelung

Balanced Angulation

- **Good angulation** facilitates a smooth ground-covering stride.
- **Balance** facilitates good foot-timing. When balanced, thrust from the rear quarters is transmitted smoothly and without loss of power to the forequarters.
- **Balanced angles create efficient movement** which is necessary for the stamina to work all day.

Out of Balance

More rear angulation than front angulation. When moving, the rear foot reaches past the front foot causing the dog to twist his body to avoid stepping on his own feet. He's not able to move with his front and rear legs in a parallel plane of travel, his body moves at an angle to the line of travel, which is called crabbing. A dog should not crab; his spine should be straight and pointed in the direction of travel.

More front angulation than rear angulation. When shoulder angulation is greater than rear angulation the dog won't be able to maintain an even flowing gait. He will will fall heavily on the forehand won't be able to maintain a good topline. This type of movement is exhausting for the dog.

UNAUSGEGLICHENE WINKELUNGEN

Ausgewogene Winkelung

- Eine gute Winkelung ermöglicht einen effizienten raumgreifenden Schritt.
- Balance ermöglicht ein gutes Fuß-Timing. Im Gleichgewicht wird der Schub von der Hinterhand sanft und ohne Kraftverlust auf die Vorderhand übertragen.
- Ausgewogene Winkel sorgen für eine effiziente Bewegung, die für die Ausdauer erforderlich ist, um den ganzen Tag zu arbeiten.

Aus dem Gleichgewicht

Mehr Hinterhandwinkelung als Vorderhandwinkelung. Bei der Bewegung reicht der Abdruck des Hinterfusses über den des Vorderfusses hinaus, wodurch der Hund seinen Körper seitwärts bewegt, um sich nicht auf die eigenen Füße zu treten. Er ist nicht in der Lage, sich mit seinen Vorder- und Hinterbeinen in einer parallelen Bewegungsebene zu bewegen, sein Körper bewegt sich schräg zur Bewegungslinie, was als Krebsgang bezeichnet wird. Ein Hund sollte sich niemals im Krebsgang vorwärts bewegen, seine Wirbelsäule sollte gerade sein und in Bewegungsrichtung zeigen.

Mehr Vorderhandwinkelung als Hinterhandwinkelung. Wenn die Schulterwinkelung größer als die Hinterhandwinkelung, kann der Hund keinen gleichmäßigen, fließenden Gang beibehalten. Er wird stark auf die Vorhand fallen und nicht in der Lage sein, eine gute Oberlinie zu halten. Diese Art der Bewegung ist für den Hund anstrengend und damit uneffizient.

ELISABETH EKNES PHOTOGRAPHY

Coat
Moderate and Easy Care

Haarkleid
Moderat und Pflegeleicht

Like
THIS

Wie das

Hair of medium texture, straight to wavy, weather resistant and of medium length.

- The undercoat varies in quantity with variations in climate.

- Hair is short and smooth on the head, ears, front of forelegs and below the hocks.

- Backs of forelegs and breeches are moderately feathered.

- There is a moderate mane and frill, more pronounced in dogs than in bitches.

MAS: Moderation is the overall impression of the coat. Trimming should be minimal. Hair may be trimmed on the ears, feet, back of hocks, pasterns, and tail, otherwise he is to be shown in a natural coat. Untrimmed whiskers are preferred.

AUSSIES: Trimming of coat and whiskers is not defined.

AUSSIES AND MAS: SEVERE FAULT: Non-typical coats.

HAARKLEID

Das Haarkleid vermittelt insgesamt einen moderaten Eindruck.

- Das Haar ist von mittlerer Struktur, gerade bis wellig, wetterfest und von mittlerer Länge.

- Der Anteil des Unterhaares variiert abhängig von den klimatischen Bedingungen.

- Am Kopf und an den Vorderseiten der Läufe ist das Haar kurz und glatt.

- Die Hinterseiten der Vorderläufe und die Hosen sind moderat befedert. Bei Rüden sind Mähne und Kragen moderat und ausgeprägter als bei Hündinnen.

MAS: Das Haar kann an den Ohren, Pfoten, Rückseite der Sprunggelenke, Hintermittelfüßen und an der Rute getrimmt werden, sonst muss es als natürliches Haarkleid getragen werden. Ungetrimmte Tasthaare werden bevorzugt.

AUSSIES UND MAS: SCHWERER FEHLER: Nicht typisches Haarkleid.

Not THAT

Diese Haarkleid sind nicht richtig

Excessively long

Overabundant, profuse

Wiry or curly

ASCA: Non-typical coats such as excessively long; over-abundant/profuse; wiry; or curly.
ASCA: Nicht typisches Haarkleid , z. B. übermäßig lang, übermäßig üppig/prollig, drahtig oder lockig.

AUSSIES AND MAS: SEVERE FAULT: Non-typical coats. / **AUSSIES UND MAS: SCHWERER FEHLER:** Nicht typisches Haarkleid.

Coats should be serviceable and low-maintenance.

These breeds were developed to work livestock on all terrain and in all weather conditions. Their coats should be low maintenance, protect them from the elements, and be self-cleaning: after getting wet and/or dirty, a correct coat dries rapidly and the dirt literally falls off.

Undercoat: Dogs in cold climates will grow more undercoat than dogs in warmer climates but the length of the top coat doesn't change.

Mane, frill and feathering: Less coat collects less mud and dirt and is easier to maintain.

HAARKLEID

Haarkleid sollen Gebrauchsfähig und pflegeleicht sein

Diese Rassen wurden entwickelt, um Vieh in jedem Gelände und bei allen Wetterbedingungen zu arbeiten. Ihr Fell sollte pflegeleicht sein, es vor Witterungseinflüssen schützen und selbstreinigend sein: Nach Nässe und/oder Verschmutzung trocknet ein richtiges Fell schnell und der Schmutz fällt buchstäblich ab.

Unterwolle: Bei Hunden in kalten Klimazonen wächst mehr Unterwolle als bei Hunden in wärmeren Klimazonen. Die Länge des Deckhaars ändert sich jedoch nicht.

Mähne, Hosen und Befederung: Weniger Fell sammelt weniger Schlamm und Schmutz und ist pflegeleichter.

COURTNEY HUTHER PHOTOGRAPHY

Colours
Gorgeous Variety

Farben
Wunderschöne Vielfalt

Like THIS

Wie das

NOELLE HOORNEMAN PHOTOGRAPHY

Black

ELISABETH EKNES PHOTOGRAPHY

Blue Merle

SASCHA VADAGNIN PHOTOGRAPHY

Red / Liver

DIANNE PHELPS PHOTOGRAPHY

Red Merle

AUSSIES: Blue merle, black, red merle, red—all with or without white markings and/or tan markings with no order of preference.

MAS: Black, blue merle, red, liver, and red or liver merle. Undercoats may be somewhat lighter in colour than the topcoat.

VIER FARBEN

AUSSIES: Bluemerle, schwarz, Redmerle, Rot, alle mit oder ohne weiße Abzeichen und / oder kupferfarbenen Abzeichen; keine Farbe soll vor der anderen vorgezogen werden.

MAS: Schwarz, Blue merle, Rot, Leberfarben, und Red merle oder Leberfarben merle. Die Unterwolle kann etwas heller sein als das Deckhaar.

Like
THIS

Wie das

BLACK TRICOLOUR

BLACK TRICOLOUR

SOLID BLACK

BLACK & WHITE BICOLOUR

BLACK & WHITE BICOLOUR

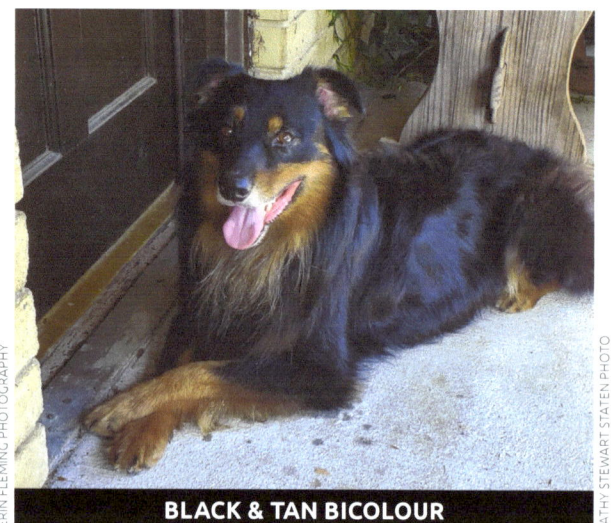
BLACK & TAN BICOLOUR

Colour can be black with white markings and tan points (black tri-colour), solid black, black with white markings (black bi-colour), or black with tan points (black bi-colour). There is no order of preference.

FARBE: SCHWARZ

Die Farbe kann einfarbig schwarz, schwarz mit weißen Abzeichen (zweifarbig/bi), schwarz mit kupferfarbenen Abzeichen (zweifarbig/bi) oder schwarz mit weißen und kupferfarbenen Abzeichen (dreifarbig/tri) sein. Es gibt keine Präferenz der Farben.

Like
THIS
Wie das

LIGHT BLUE MERLE TRICOLOUR

MEDIUM BLUE MERLE TRICOLOUR

DARK BLUE MERLE TRICOLOUR

MINIMAL BLUE MERLE BICOLOUR

HEAVILY MERLED BLUE BICOLOUR

STEEL GRAY BLUE BICOLOUR

Colours range from light blue to dark steel gray with any amount of marbling, flecks, or blotches. They may have white markings and/or tan points. There is no order of preference. It is characteristic that blue merle dogs darken with age.

FARBE: BLUE MERLE

Die Farben reichen von hellem merle bis zu dunklem Stahlgrau mit jeder Menge Marmorierungen oder Flecken. Sie können weiße und/oder kupferfarbene Abzeichen aufweisen. Es gibt keine Präferenz der Farben. Es ist charakteristisch, dass blue merle farbene Hund mit zunehmendem Alter dunkler werden.

Like THIS

Wie das

RED TRICOLOUR

RED TRICOLOUR

RED TRICOLOUR

RED TRICOLOUR

RED & TAN BICOLOUR

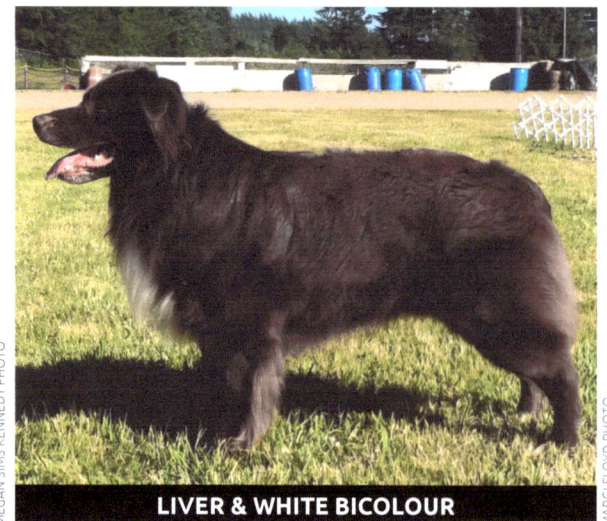
LIVER & WHITE BICOLOUR

Colour can be red with white markings and tan points (red tri-colour), solid red, red with white markings (red bi-colour), or red with tan points (red bi-colour). There is no order of preference.

FARBE: ROT / LEBER

Farbe kann einfarbig rot, rot mit weißen Anzeichen (zweifarbig/bi), rot mit kupferfarbenen Abzeichen (zweifarbig/bi) oder rot mit weißen und kupferfarbenen Abzeichen (dreifarbig/tri) sein. Die Rottöne reichen von leberfarben bis zimtrot. Es gibt keine Präferenz der Farben.

Like
THIS

Wie das

RED MERLE TRICOLOUR

LIVER RED MERLE TRICOLOUR

HEAVILY MERLED RED TRICOLOUR

RED MERLE TRICOLOUR

RED MERLE & WHITE BICOLOUR

RED MERLE & WHITE BICOLOUR

Colours range from deep liver to cinnamon red with any amount of marbling, flecks, or blotches.
They may have white markings and/or tan points. There is no order of preference.

FARBE: ROT / LEBER MERLE

Die Farbtöne reichen von leberfarben bis zimtrot mit jeder Menge Marmorierungen oder Flecken. Sie können weiße und/oder kupferfarbene Markierungen aufweisen. Es gibt keine Präferenz der Farben.

Like
THIS

Alle sind akzeptabel

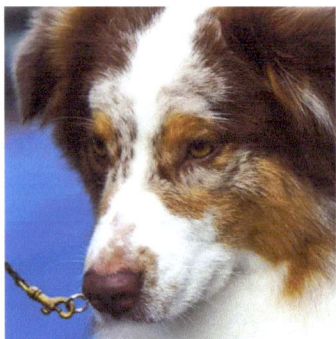

DIANA FALCONER PHOTOGRAPHY

HOLLY REGINA PRESS PHOTOGRAPHY

DEBBY MICHIELSEN PHOTO

Minimal merling. *This colouring is correct.*

The only merling on the red dog is on her face. The rest of her body is solid red. She is genetically a red merle and can produce merle offspring if crossed with a solid colour dog. The puppy has merling only on his face, throat, and chest. He is genetically a blue merle.

MINIMALER MERLING

Diese Farbe ist korrekt.

Der einzige Merlefärbung an dem roten Hund ist in seinem Gesicht. Der Rest ihres Körpers is einfarbig rot. Sie ist genetisch ein Red Merle und kann Merle-Nachkommen produzieren, wenn sie mit einem einfarbigen Hund verpaart wird. Der Welpe hat Merling nur im Gesicht, am Hals und an der Brust. Er ist genetisch ein Blue Merle.

WOJTECKI PHOTO

Uneven merling.

This colouring is correct.

The two photos above picture dogs with irregularly distributed merling patches, which is correct and equally as desirable as a coat with more evenly distributed merling patches.

UNGLEICHMÄSSIGE FÄRBUNG
Diese Farbe ist korrekt.

Die beiden Fotos oben zeigen Hunde mit unregelmäßig verteilten Merling-Flecken, was korrekt und ebenso wünschenswert ist wie ein Fell mit gleichmäßig verteilten Merling-Flecken.

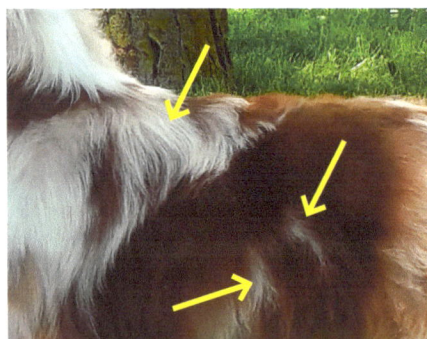

BRANDI CAREY PHOTO

Three areas of merling, not white.

Drei Schattierungen von merle – nicht weiß.

Light colour merling. *This colouring is correct.*

Merling can be very light in colour, appearing almost white, as shown on the dog at left. If there is doubt, slide a white piece of paper under the gray hair to compare it to true white.

HELLER FARBMERLING

Diese Farbe ist korrekt.

Merle kann ein sehr helle Farbe haben und fast weiß erscheinen. Wenn Sie Zweifel haben, schieben Sie ein weißes Blatt Papier unter das graue Haar, um es mit echtem Weiß zu vergleichen.

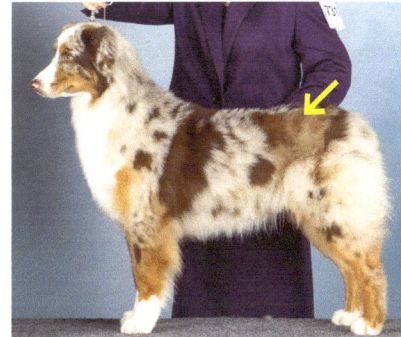

Dilution spots on blue merles. / Dilution spots auf Blue Merles.

Dilution spots on red merles. / Dilution spots auf Red Merles.

Dilution spots on merles are NOT genetically the same as dilute colour. *See page 63.*

Dilution spots are isolated off-colour areas in an otherwise normally-coloured merle coat. They can be small or can cover large areas.

On blue merles, dilution spots can be shades of brown or dusty gray. A rusty brown dilution spot does not mean a blue merle dog is red factored (carries the red gene), which is a common misconception.

On red merles, dilution spots are intermediate shades of red/liver.

Some of the dogs pictured on this page may be tweed or harlequin patterned merles, a trait that can be inherited independently from the merle gene.

There is probably a degree of inheritance of dilution spots, so this trait should be considered when choosing breeding pairs.

Dilution spots are cosmetic and do not affect a dog's ability to do his job, nor do they have any negative effects on his health, but they are a deviation from the ideal.

DILUTION SPOTS AUF MERLES

Dilution Spots auf Merles sind genetisch NICHT mit der Farbverdünnung (dilute) gleichzusetzen. *Page 63.*

Dilution Spots sind isolierte fehlfarbige Bereiche in einem ansonsten normal gefärbten Merle-Fell. Sie können klein sein oder große Flächen bedecken.

Bei Blue Merles können Dilution Spots braune oder staubgraue Schattierungen aufweisen. Ein rostbrauner Verdünnungsfleck bedeutet nicht, dass ein Blue-Merle-Hund red factored ist (das rote Gen trägt), was ein weit verbreiteter Irrglaube ist.

Bei Red Merles sind die Dilution Spots Zwischenstufen von Rot/Leber.

Einige der auf dieser Seite abgebildeten Hunde sind möglicherweise Tweed- oder Harlekin-gemusterte Merles, ein Merkmal, das unabhängig vom Merle-Gen vererbt werden kann.

Dilution Spots werden wahrscheinlich bis zu einem gewissen Grad vererbt, daher sollte dieses Merkmal bei der Auswahl des Zuchtpartners berücksichtigt werden.

Dilution Spots sind kosmetischer Natur und beeinträchtigen weder die Fähigkeit des Hundes, seine Arbeit zu verrichten, noch haben sie negative Auswirkungen auf seine Gesundheit, aber sie sind eine Abweichung vom Ideal.

AUSSIES:

With or without white markings and/or tan markings, with no order of preference.

MAS:

Tan markings are not required but when present are acceptable in any or all of the following areas: around the eyes, on the feet, legs, chest, muzzle, underside of neck, face, underside of ear, underline of body, under the base of the tail and the breeches.

Tan markings vary in shades from creamy beige to dark rust, with no preference. Asymmetrical markings are not to be faulted. Blending with the base colour or merle pattern may be present on the face, legs, feet, and breeches.

LOHFARBENE ABZEICHEN

AUSSIES:

Mit mit oder ohne weiße Abzeichen und / oder kupferfarbenen Abzeichen

MAS:

Lohfarbene Abzeichen sind nicht erforderlich, werden jedoch in allen der folgenden Bereiche akzeptiert: Um die Augen, an Pfoten, Läufen, Brust, Nasenschwamm, Halsunterseite, Gesicht, Ohrunterseite, untere Profillinie des Körpers, unter der Rutenwurzel und an den Hosen. Lohfarbene Abzeichen variieren in Schattierungen von creme Beige bis dunkler Rost, ohne Präferenzen. Übergang in die Grundfarbe oder das Merle-Muster im Gesicht, an den Läufen, Pfoten und Hosen.

LEENA KOIVUNEN PHOTOGRAPHY

LINDA KEOGH PHOTO

ANN SHOPE PHOTO

THORNAPPLE PHOTO

PETER LINDSAY PHOTO

Not THAT

Nicht das

Yellow

Sable

Dilute Black

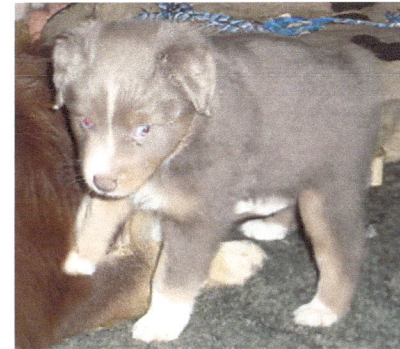
Dilute Red

AUSSIES: FAULT
MAS: DISQUALIFICATION: Other than recognized colours.

YELLOW can be mistaken for light red. A Palomino-colour dog with a black nose is definitely yellow. A Palomino-colour dog with a liver nose is difficult to differentiate from a red dog without genetic testing. Yellow dogs do not have tan trim and can have hidden merling.

SABLE colour has reddish hair shafts that are tipped in black (black nose) or tipped in liver (liver nose). There can be varying amounts of darker shading over the base coat colour and they can have hidden merling. Sables with liver noses can appear to be yellow or normal red.

DILUTE BLACK and **DILUTE RED** coats (which are NOT the same as dilution spots) are very common in both solids and merles. The gray puppy above is a black tricolour but the dilution gene causes his coat to be gray. Dilute red resembles the dusky pink colour of a Weimaraner. All dilute colours can have normal tan and white trim.

WHY are non-standard colours faulted or disqualified?

Non-standard colours detract significantly from breed character and may indicate mongrelization.

Yellow and **sable** can mask the presence of the merle gene. If a person didn't realize their yellow or sable dog carried a merle gene and they bred it to a typical merle, some of the offspring could be blind or deaf because they would have two copies of the merle gene.

There are DNA tests available to determine genotype for dilute, yellow, sable, and other colours.

NICHT-STANDARD FARBEN

AUSSIES: FEHLER
MAS: DISQUALIFIKATION: Andere als die anerkannten Farben.

YELLOW kann mit Hellrot verwechselt werden. Ein palominofarbener Hund mit schwarzer Nase ist definitiv yellow. Ein palominofarbener Hund mit Lebernase ist ohne Gentests schwer von einem Roten zu unterscheiden. Yellow Hunde haben keine lohfarbene Abzeichen und können versteckt das Merlegen tragen.

SABLE hat rötliche Haarschäfte, die schwarze (schwarze Nase) oder leberfarbene (leberfarbene Nase) Spitzen haben. Es können unterschiedliche Mengen dunklerer Schattierungen über der vorhanden sein und sie können versteckte Verschmelzungen aufweisen. Sable mit Lebernasen können yellow oder normal rot erscheinen.

DILUTE BLACK und **DILUTE RED** bei Einfarbigen als auch in Merles sehr verbreitet. Der graue Hund oben ist schwarz, aber das Verdünnungsgen bewirkt, dass sein Fell grau ist. Verdünntes Rot ähnelt der dunkelrosa Farbe eines Weimaraners. Alle verdünnten Farben können normale lohfarbene Abzeichen haben.

WARUM werden Nicht-Standard Farben bemängelt oder disqualifiziert?

Nicht-Standard Farben beeinträchtigen den Charakter der Rasse erheblich und können auf eine Vermischung hinweisen.

Yellow und **Sable** können das Vorhandensein des Merle-Gens verdecken. Wenn eine Person nicht weiß, dass ihr gelber oder zobelner Hund ein Merle-Gen trägt und sie ihn mit einem typischen Merle verpaart, könnten einige der Nachkommen blind oder taub sein, da sie zwei Kopien des Merle-Gens haben würden.

Es stehen DNA-Tests zur Verfügung, um den Genotyp für dilute, yellow und sable zu bestimmen.

Like THIS

Wie das

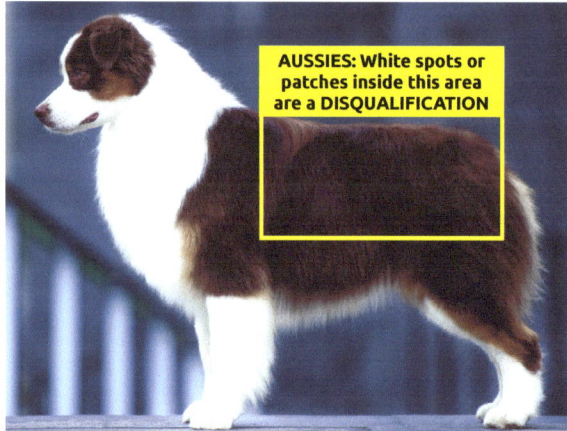

AUSSIES: White spots or patches inside this area are a DISQUALIFICATION

MAS: Conspicuous, isolated spot or patch of white inside this area is a DISQUALIFICATION

AUSSIES: Acceptable white collar and an acceptable amount of stifle white with very little belly white.

AUSSIES: Weiß in diesem Bereich ist eine Disqualifikation. Dieser Aussie hat einen akzeptablen weißen Kragen und einen akzeptablen Anteil weiß am Knie und sehr wenig weiß am Bauch.

MAS: Acceptable white collar and an acceptable amount of belly and stifle white.

MAS: Auffälliger, isolierter Fleck oder weißer Fleck in diesem Bereich ist eine Disqualifikation. Dieser MAS hat einen akzeptablen weißen Kragen und einen akzeptablen Anteil weiß an Bauch und Knie.

AUSSIES: Maximum acceptable belly white.
MAS: FAULT. Exceeds 1 inch (2.5 cm) above elbow.

AUSSIES: Akzeptabel Weiß am Bauch.
MAS: FEHLER. Mehr als 2,5 cm (1 Zoll) über dem Ellbogen.

White coming up from the underpart (belly and stifle white)

AUSSIES: White extension from underpart up to 4 inches (10 cm) measuring from a horizontal line at the elbow.

MAS: A thin outline of white extension on the stifle. A small amount of white extending from the underline may be visible from the side, not to exceed 1 inch (2.5 cm) above the elbow.

If a dog appears to have excess white coming up from the underpart, lift up the hair and verify the location of the **root** of the hair. The root of the hair must not extend into the body colour.

NOTE: Look at both sides of the dog because markings can be different.

AKZEPTABLE WEISSE MARKIERUNGEN

Weiß kommt von der Unterseite hoch (Bauch und Knie weiß)

AUSSIES: Weiße Verlängerung von einer horizontalen Linie in Ellenbogenhöhe an gemessen, darf sich bis zu einer Länge von 10 cm (4 Inches) ausdehnen.

MAS: Ein geringer Anteil Weiß von der unteren Profillinie kann von der Seite sichtbar sein, darf jedoch nicht mehr als 2,5 cm (1 Zoll) über den Ellbogen reichen.

Wenn bei einem Hund zu viel Weiß von der Unterlinie in den Körper ragt, heben Sie das Haar an und überprüfen Sie die Lage der Haarwurzel. Die Haarwurzel darf nicht in die Körperfarbe hineinragen.

Sehen Sie sich beide Seiten des Hundes an, da die Abzeichen unterschiedlich sein können.

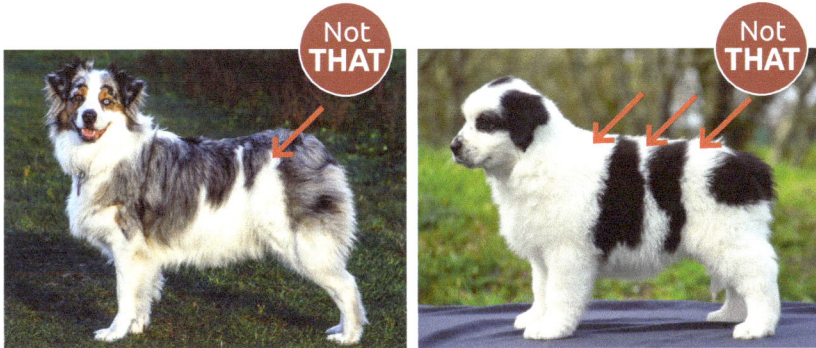

Excess Body White / Übermäßiges Weiß am Körper

AUSSIES and **MAS:** FAULTED to degree of deviation from the ideal.

AUSSIES und **MAS:** FEHLER nach dem Grad der Abweichung vom Ideal.

White Body Splash / Weiße Flecken am Körper

AUSSIES and **MAS:** DISQUALIFICATION: Isolated white body splash.

AUSSIES und **MAS:** DISQUALIFIKATION: Isolierte weiße Flecken am Körper.

WHY are white body splashes disqualified and excess body and head white undesirable?

White outside of the areas described in the standards is a warning sign that there may be health problems related to lack of pigment. Excess white can be produced by several gene combinations.

- Puppies from a **merle to merle cross** that have excess white markings are frequently blind and fully or partially deaf.
- Puppies from a **solid to merle cross** that have excess white markings may have two copies of the Piebald or other white spotting genes that can be associated with deafness, particularly if there is white around the base of the ear.

DEFINITION: White body splashes

AUSSIES: White body splashes in all colours, which means [isolated] white on the body between withers and tail, on sides between elbows and back of hindquarters.

MAS: White body splashes, which means any conspicuous, isolated spot or patch of white on the area between withers and tail, on back, or sides between elbows and back of hindquarters.

ÜBERSCHÜSSIGES WEIß AM KÖRPER UND WEIßE FLECKEN

WARUM werden Weiße Flecken disqualifiziert und von Übermäßigem Weiß am Körper und Kopf unerwünscht?

Weiß außerhalb der in den Standards beschriebenen Bereiche ist ein Warnsignal, das auf gesundheitliche Probleme im Zusammenhang mit Pigmentmangel hinweisen kann. Überschüssiges Weiß kann durch verschiedene Genkombinationen erzeugt werden.

- Welpen aus einer Merle-Merle-Kreuzung, die übermäßig weiße Abzeichen aufweisen, sind häufig blind und ganz oder teilweise taub.
- Welpen aus einer einfarbigen x merle Verpaarung können übermäßiges Weiß aufweisen, sie können zwei Kopien des Piebald-Gens oder anderer Gene für weiße Flecken haben, die mit Taubheit in Verbindung gebracht werden können, insbesondere wenn das Weiß um den Ohransatz platziert ist.

DEFINITION: Weiße Flecken am Körper

AUSSIES UND MAS: Weiße Flecken am Körper, das heißt, auffälliger, isolierter weißer Fleck oder Platte im Bereich zwischen Widerrist und Rute, auf dem Rücken oder an den Seiten zwischen den Ellbogen und der Hinterseite der Hinterläufe.

The *hairline* of a white collar should not exceed the point of the withers at the skin.

AUSSIES AND MAS: **FAULT**

Die Haarlinie des weißen Kragens reicht nicht über den Widerrist an der Haut hinaus.

AUSSIES UND MAS: **FEHLER**

Wie das

Nicht das

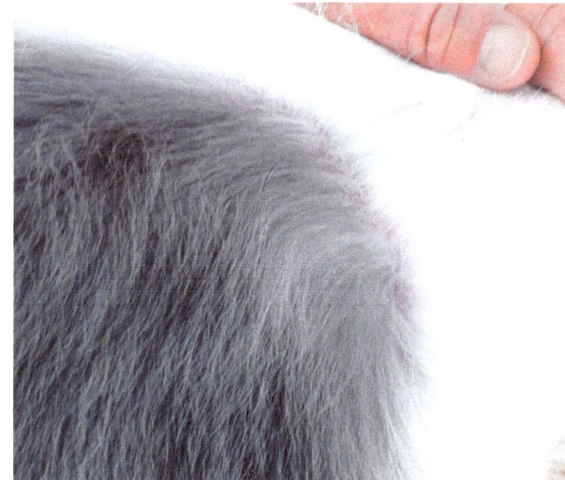

White collar

The hairline (root) of the white collar should not exceed the point of the withers. Lift the coat to see the roots.

Weißer Kragen

Die Haarlinie des weißen Kragens reicht nicht über den Widerrist an der Haut hinaus. Heben Sie das Haar an und überprüfen Sie die Lage der Haarwurzel.

Hands-on examination

If the white collar of a dog *appears* to extend past the point of the withers, it's important to examine the collar with your hands. Lift up the hair and verify the location of the *root* of the hair. The *root* of the collar hair must not extend past the point of the withers into the body colour. A hands-on exam reveals that the white collar of the above dog does *not* exceed the point of the withers and is acceptable according to the standard.

However, the white on the dog at lower left exceeds the point of the withers and has excess white on other parts of its body. More information on page 65.

WEIßER KRAGEN

Praktische Prüfung

Wenn der weiße Kragen eines Hundes über den Widerrist hinausragt, ist es wichtig, den Kragen mit den Händen zu untersuchen. Heben Sie das Haar an und überprüfen Sie die Lage der Haarwurzel. Die Kragenhaarwurzel darf nicht über die Widerristspitze hinaus in die Körperfarbe hineinragen. Eine praktische Prüfung zeigt, dass der weiße Kragen des oben genannten Hundes die Widerristspitze nicht überschreitet und gemäß dem Standard akzeptabel ist.

Das Weiß des Hundes unten links überschreitet jedoch die Widerristspitze und weist an anderen Körperteilen überschüssiges Weiß auf.

WEIß AM KOPF

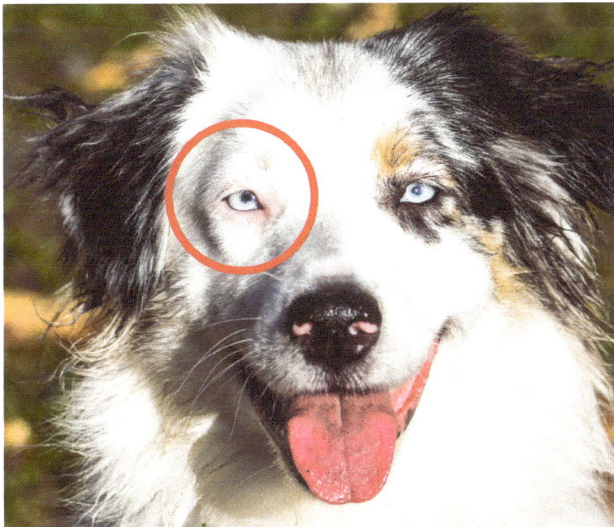

White on ears

AUSSIES: White on the head should not predominate.

MAS: Ears fully covered by colour are preferred.
SEVERE FAULT: White markings covering over 25% of an ear.

WHY?
White surrounding the ears can predispose dogs to deafness. If the hair cells in the inner ear lack pigment, the nerve endings will atrophy and die in the first few weeks of life and full or partial deafness will result. However, many dogs with white ears have normal hearing.

Weiß an den Ohren

AUSSIES: Im Standard wird Weiß an den Ohren nicht ausdrücklich erwähnt.
MAS: Bevorzugt werden vollständig von Farbe bedeckte Ohren. **SCHWERE FEHLER:** Weiße Abzeichen, die mehr als 25 Prozent eines Ohres bedecken.

WARUM? Eine weiße Umgebung der Ohren kann Hunde für Taubheit prädisponieren. Wenn den Haarzellen im Innenohr das Pigment fehlt, verkümmern die Nervenenden und sterben in den ersten Lebenswochen ab, was zu vollständiger oder teilweiser Taubheit führt. Viele Hunde mit weißen Ohren haben jedoch ein normales Gehör.

White should not surround eyes

AUSSIES AND MAS: Eyes must be fully surrounded by colour and pigment.
WHY? White colour around the eyes may indicate eye defects resulting from improper development of the tissues of the eye. **This applies to puppies from a merle to merle pairing.**

Weiß sollte die Augen nicht umgeben

AUSSIES UND MAS: Das Weiß ist am Kopf nicht vorherrschend und die Augen sind vollständig von Farbe und Pigmentierung umgeben.

WARUM? Weiße Farbe um die Augen kann auf Augenfehler hinweisen, die auf eine unsachgemäße Entwicklung des Augengewebes zurückzuführen sind. **Dies gilt für Welpen aus einer Merle zu Merle Verpaarung.**

Not THAT

Faults
Severe Faults
Disqualfications

Fehler
Schwere Fehler
Disqualifizierende Fehler

Not THAT

Nicht das

FAULTS

AUSSIES:
Any departure from the foregoing points should be considered a fault and the seriousness with which the fault should be regarded should be in exact proportion to its degree and its effect upon the health and welfare of the dog.

MAS:
Any departure from the foregoing points should be considered a fault and the seriousness with which the fault should be regarded should be in exact proportion to its degree and its effect upon the health and welfare of the dog and its ability to perform its traditional work.

FEHLER

AUSSIES:
Jede Abweichung von den vorgenannten Punkten muss als Fehler angesehen werden, dessen Bewertung in genauem Verhältnis zum Grad der Abweichung stehen sollte und dessen Einfluss auf die Gesundheit und das Wohlbefinden des Hundes.

MAS:
Jede Abweichung von den vorgenannten Punkten muss als Fehler angesehen werden, dessen Bewertung in genauem Verhältnis zum Grad der Abweichung stehen sollte und dessen Einfluss auf die Gesundheit und das Wohlbefinden des Hundes und seine Fähigkeit, die verlangte rassetypische Arbeit zu erbringen, zu beachten ist.

SEVERE FAULTS / SCHWERE FEHLER

SEVERE FAULT: EARS
AUSSIES and **MAS:** Prick ears and hanging ears.

SCHWERE FEHLER
AUSSIES und **MAS:** Stehohren oder Hängeohren.

SEVERE FAULT: NOSE PIGMENT
MAS: Between 25 and 50% unpigmented nose leather.

SCHWERE FEHLER
MAS: Zwischen 25 und 50% unpigmentiertes Nasenleder.

SEVERE FAULT: COAT
AUSSIES and **MAS:** Non-typical coats.

SCHWERE FEHLER
AUSSIES und **MAS:** Untypisches Haarkleid.

SEVERE FAULT: WHITE ON EARS
MAS: White markings covering over 25% of an ear.

SCHWERE FEHLER
MAS: Weiße Abzeichen, die mehr als 25% eines Ohrs bedecken.

DISQUALIFYING FAULTS / DISQUALIFIZIERENDE FEHLER

DISQUALIFICATION: TEMPERAMENT

AUSSIES and **MAS:**
- Aggressive or overly shy.
- Any dog clearly showing physical or behavioural abnormalities.

DISQUALIFIKATION

AUSSIES und **MAS:**
- Aggressive oder übermäßig ängstliche Hunde.
- Hunde, die deutlich physische Abnormitäten oder Verhaltensstörungen aufweisen.

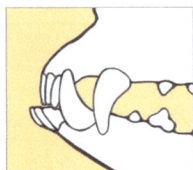

DISQUALIFICATION: BITE

AUSSIES and **MAS:** Undershot bite.

DISQUALIFIKATION

AUSSIES und **MAS:** Vorbiß.

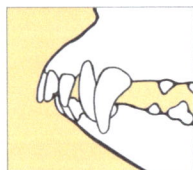

AUSSIES: Overshot bite by more than ⅛ inch.
MAS: Overshot bite.

DISQUALIFIKATION

AUSSIES: Rückbiß mit mehr als ⅛ inch (2.5 mm).
MAS: Überbiss.

DISQUALIFICATION: WHITE BODY SPLASH

AUSSIES and **MAS:** White body splashes.

DISQUALIFIKATION

AUSSIES und **MAS:** Weiße Flecken am Körper.

DISQUALIFICATION: SIZE

MAS: SIZE
- Dogs under 35.5 cm and over 46 cm.
- Bitches under 33 cm and over 43.5 cm.

DISQUALIFIKATION

MAS: GRÖSSE
- Rüde unter 35,5 cm und über 46 cm.
- Hündinnen unter 33 cm und über 43,5 cm.

DISQUALIFICATION: NOSE PIGMENT

MAS: Over 50% un-pigmented nose leather.

DISQUALIFIKATION

MAS: Mehr als 50% fehlende Pigmentierung am Nasenschwamm.

DISQUALIFICATION: COLOUR

MAS: Other than recognized colours: Dilute black, Dilute red, Yellow, Sable

DISQUALIFIKATION

MAS: Andere als die anerkannten Farben. Dilute black, Dilute red, Yellow, Sable

N.B. (*Nota Bene:* please note)
- Male animals should have two apparently normal testicles fully descended into the scrotum.
- Only functionally and clinically healthy dogs, with breed typical conformation, should be used for breeding.

- Rüden müssen zwei offensichtlich normal entwickelte Hoden aufweisen, die sich vollständig im Hodensack befinden.
- Zur Zucht sollen ausschließlich funktional und klinisch gesunde, rassetypische Hunde verwendet werden.

Empfehlungen für Richter

PROPORTIONEN

- Eine moderate Struktur ist wichtig bei Erhaltung des Rassetyps und rassetypischen Kopfes/Ausdrucks – bedeutet aber nicht mittelmäßig!
- Moderat bedeutet die Beseitigung oder Reduzierung von Extremen.
- Denken Sie daran: etwas länger als hoch – das richtige Verhältnis von Körperlänge zu Körpergröße beträgt 10:9.
- Größe: Aussies gibt es in einer Vielzahl von Größen ohne Disqualifikation; wählen Sie nach Qualität und nicht nach Größe. Größe ist ein disqualifizierender Fehler für MAS.
- Vermeiden Sie es, Hunde mit falschen Proportionen und Bewegungen zu belohnen.
- Belohnen sie nicht lang und niedrig, was die Ausdauer verringert.

BEWEGUNG

- Bewegung: Auch hier ist Mäßigung wichtig, diese Hunde brauchen die Ausdauer, um den ganzen Tag zu arbeiten.
- Geschmeidig, frei und leicht, gut ausbalanciert mit einem bodendeckenden Schritt. Sie sind leicht auf den Beinen und zeigen wenig oder keine Anstrengung. Ausgewogenheit ist wichtig! Kommen, Gehen und Seitengangwerk sind gleichberechtigt.
- Suchen Sie nach fitten Hunden mit gutem Gewicht und Muskeltonus.
- Übermäßiges Tempo und ein hoch getragener Kopf in der Bewegung sollten nicht belohnt werden.

KOPF

- Suchen Sie nach den richtigen Kopfdetails. Große, schwere Ohren und lose Lippen sind nicht erwünscht.

GROOMING

- Übermäßiges Grooming sollte nicht belohnt werden. Wenn Sie Scherenspuren oder gerade Schnittlinien auf den Haaren sehen können, ist dies zu viel. Die Hunde sollten auf natürliche Weise ausgestellt werden. Das Trimmen von Ohren, Füßen, Sprunggelenken und Rute ist akzeptabel; Schneiden am Körper sind diese natürlichen Arbeitsrassen falsch.

TYP

- Sie werden viele Variationen des Rassetyps finden – was für diese Rassen in Ordnung ist.

EINSTELLUNG

- Nicht alle Aussies und MAS lieben den Showring. Ihr Hund von bester Qualität ist möglicherweise nicht der lebhafteste. Wählen Sie Qualität vor Showmanship.

FARBE

- Färbungen und Markierungen können optische Täuschungen erzeugen, also verwenden Sie im Zweifelsfall Ihre Hände zur Überprüfung.

Asymmetrische Markierungen an Beinen und Brust können das Auge täuschen. Im Zweifelsfall mit den Händen untersuchen.

16. 06. 2010/ DE
FCI - Standard Nr. 342

Australian Shepherd (Australischer Schäferhund)

Übersetzung : Dr. J-M. Paschoud und Frau R. Binder.
Ergänzung, Christina Bailey / Offizielle Originalsprache (EN)
Ursprung : U.S.A.
Datum der publikation des Gültigen Original-Standardes : 26.03. 2009.
Verwendung : Farm und Ranch Hűtehund
Klassifikation FCI: Gruppe 1 Hütehunde und Treibhunde (ausgenommen Schweizer Sennenhunde) Sektion 1 Schäferhunde Ohne Arbeitsprüfung.

KURZER GESCHICHTLICHER ABRISS:

Obschon es zahlreiche Theorien über den Ursprung des Australischen Schäferhundes gibt, wissen wir heute, dass diese Rasse sich ausschließlich in den USA entwickelt hat. Er hat den Namen Australischer Schäferhund erhalten, weil angenommen wird, dass um 1800 baskische Schafhirten bei ihrer Einwanderung von Australien nach Amerika diese Hunde mitbrachten.

Die Beliebtheit des Australischen Schäferhundes nahm nach dem zweiten Weltkrieg parallel zur schnellen Entwicklung der Western-Reiterei zu, welche durch Rodeos, Pferderennen, Kino- und Televisionsberichte allgemein bekannt und volkstümlich wurde. Seine vielfachen Begabungen und die Leichtigkeit, ihn auszubilden machten ihn zu einem nützlichen Zubehör für Ranches und Farmen in Amerika. Die Farmer in den USA sorgten für die Weiterentwicklung der Rasse und die Erhaltung seiner vorteilbringenden Eigenschaften, seiner scharfen Intelligenz, seines ausgesprochenen Herdentriebes sowie seines attraktiven Erscheinungsbildes, welches schon ursprünglich die Bewunderung aller auf sich gezogen hatte.

Obschon jeder einzelne Hund ein Unikum in Farbe und Zeichnung darstellt, zeigen alle Australischen Schäferhunde eine unübertreffbare Anhänglichkeit gegenüber ihrem Meister und seiner Familie. Seine zahlreichen guten Eigenschaften haben seine stetige Beliebtheit aufrechterhalten.

ALLGEMEINES ERSCHEINUNGSBILD: Der Australische Schäferhund ist gut proportioniert, etwas länger als hoch und von mittlerer Größe und Knochenstärke. Die Farben seines Haarkleides haben eine große individuelle Variationsbreite. Er ist aufmerksam und lebhaft, geschmeidig und beweglich, kräftig und gut bemuskelt, jedoch ohne jede Schwere. Sein Haar ist mittellang und mäßig grob. Er hat entweder eine kupierte oder eine natürliche Stummelrute.

WICHTIGE PROPORTIONEN: Die Länge des Rumpfes (von der Brustbeinspitze zum Sitzbeinhöcker gemessen) ist etwas größer als die Widerristhöhe. Der Australische Schäferhund ist somit etwas länger als hoch.

KÖRPERBAU: Robust, Knochenstärke mäßig. Der Körperbau des Rüden ist geschlechtstypisch kräftig, ohne jedoch derb zu wirken. Die Hündin ist sehr weiblich in ihrem Aussehen, jedoch ohne jegliche Schwäche in ihrem Knochenbau.

VERHALTEN / CHARAKTER (WESEN): Der Australische Schäferhund ist ein intelligenter Arbeitshund mit ausgesprochenem Hüte- und Bewachungsinstinkt. Er ist ein pflichtgetreuer Gefährte und fähig, mit Ausdauer den ganzen Tag zu arbeiten.

Er ist charakterlich ausgeglichen und gutmütig, selten streitsüchtig. Beim ersten Kontakt mag er etwas reserviert sein.

KOPF: Mit sauberen Umrisslinien, kräftig und trocken steht der Kopf in einem guten Größenverhältnis zum Körper.

OBERKOPF :

SCHÄDEL: Das Schädeldach ist flach bis leicht gewölbt. Der Hinterhauptstachel kann etwas sichtbar sein. Die Schädellänge entspricht der Schädelbreite.

STOPP: Der Stopp ist mäßig ausgeprägt.

GESICHTSSCHÄDEL :

NASENSCHWAMM: Bei Bluemerle und bei Hunden mit schwarzem Haarkleid sind der Naschwamm und die Lippen schwarz pigmentiert, bei Redmerle und Hunden mit rotem Haarkleid leberfarben (braun). Bei den Merlehunden sind kleine rosarote Flecken zulässig. Diese sollten jedoch bei Hunden, die älter als einjährig sind, nicht mehr als 25% der Fläche des Nasenschwammes einnehmen; sonst ist es ein schwerer Fehler.

Fang Er ist gleich lang oder etwas kürzer als der Schädel. Von der Seite gesehen verlaufen die Begrenzungslinien von Schädel und Fang parallel. Der Stop ist mäßig ausgebildet, aber deutlich umrissen. Der Fang verjüngt sich nur wenig vom Ansatz bis zum Nasenschwamm und ist am Ende abgerundet.

KIEFER / ZÄHNE: Komplettes Scherengebiss mit kräftigen weißen Zähnen; Zangengebiss wird toleriert.

AUGEN: Sie sind braun, blau, bernsteinfarben oder ihre Farbe ist eine Kombination oder Variation dieser Farben, auch gefleckt oder marmoriert. Mandelförmig, weder vorstehend noch eingesunken. Die Bluemerle und die Hunde mit schwarzem Haarkleid weisen eine schwarze Augenumrandung auf; die Redmerle und die Hunde mit rotem Haarkleid zeigen eine leberfarbene (braune) Pigmentierung.

AUSDRUCK: Aufmerksam und intelligent, wachsam und lebhaft. Der Blick ist durchdringend, aber freundlich.

OHREN: Dreieckig, von mäßiger Größe und Dicke, hoch am Kopf angesetzt. Bei voller Aufmerksamkeit kippen die Ohren nach vorne oder nach der Seite wie ein Rosenohr. Stehohren und Hängeohren sind schwere Fehler.

HALS: Kräftig, von mäßiger Länge, Oberlinie leicht gewölbt. Der Hals geht harmonisch in die Schulterpartie über.

KÖRPER :

Obere Profillinie: Der Rücken ist gerade und kräftig, fest und verläuft horizontal von Widerrist bis zu den Hüften.

KRUPPE: Mäßig abfallend.

BRUST: Nicht breit, dafür aber tief: sie reicht an ihrem tiefsten Punkt bis zur Höhe der Ellenbogen.

RIPPEN: Lang und gut gewölbt; der Brustkorb ist weder tonnenförmig noch flach.

UNTERE PROFILLINIE UND BAUCH: Mäßig aufgezogen.

RUTE: Gerade, naturbelassene Länge oder mit natürlicher Stummelrute. Sofern kupiert (nur in den Ländern die kein Rutenkupierverbot erlassen haben) oder mit natürlicher Stummelrute nicht länger als 10 cm.

GLIEDMASSEN

VORDERHAND :

SCHULTER: Schulterblätter lang, flach und gut schräg gelagert; Schulterblattkuppen am Widerrist ziemlich nahe beieinanderliegend.

OBERARM: Sollte ungefähr gleich lang sein wie das Schulterblatt; er steht ungefähr in einem rechten Winkel zum Schulterblatt, mit geraden und senkrecht zu Boden stehenden Vorderläufen.

LÄUFE : Gerade und kräftig, Knochen stark und eher von ovalem als von rundem Querschnitt.

VORDERMITTELFUSS: Von mittlerer Länge, sehr leicht schräg. Afterkrallen können entfernt werden.

VORDERPFOTEN: Oval, kompakt, mit eng an einander liegenden, gut gewölbten Zehen. Ballen dick und elastisch.

HINTERHAND:

ALLGEMEINES: Die Breite der Hinterhand ist ungefähr gleich wie die der Vorderhand auf Schulterhöhe. Die Winkelung des Beckens zum Oberschenkel stimmt mit der Winkelung des Schulterblattes zum Oberarm überein und entspricht ungefähr einem rechten Winkel.

KNIEGELENK: Ausgeprägt.

SPRUNGGELENK: Mäßig gewinkelt.

HINTERMITTELFUB: Kurz, von hinten gesehen senkrecht und parallel gestellt. Afterkrallen müssen entfernt sein.

HINTERPFOTEN: Oval, kompakt, mit eng an einander liegenden, gut gewölbten Zehen. Ballen dick und elastisch.

GANGWERK: Die Gangart des australischen Schäferhundes ist geschmeidig, leicht und frei. Er ist sehr behände mit einem harmonischen, raumgreifenden Bewegungsablauf. Vorder- und Hinterläufe bewegen sich gerade und parallel zur mittleren Achse des Körpers. Bei zunehmender Geschwindigkeit nähern sich Vorder- und Hinterpfoten der mittleren Schwerpunktlinie des Körpers, während der Rücken fest und gerade bleibt. Der Australische Schäferhund muss flink und fähig sein, augenblicklich einen Richtungswechsel vorzunehmen oder ein andere Gangart einzuschlagen.

HAARKLEID

HAAR: Von mittlerer Textur, gerade bis gewellt, wetterbeständig und von mittlerer Länge. Die Dichte der Unterwolle ändert den klimatischen Bedingungen entsprechend. Das Haar ist kurz und glatt am Kopf, an den Ohren, an der Vorderseite der Vorderläufe und unterhalb der Sprunggelenke. Die Hinterseiten der Vorderläufe und die „Hosen" sind mäßig befedert. Mähne und Halskrause sind mäßig ausgebildet, bei den Rüden mehr als bei den Hündinnen. Ein atypisch beschaffenes Haarkleid ist ein schwerer Fehler.

FARBE: Bluemerle, Schwarz, Redmerle, Rot, alle mit oder ohne Weiße Abzeichen und / oder kupferfarbenen Abzeichen; keine Farbe soll vor der anderen vorgezogen werden. Die Haarlinie des weißen Kragens darf nicht weiter als bis zum Widerrist reichen.

Weiß ist zulässig am Hals ganzer oder unvollständiger Kragen), an der Brust, an den Läufen, an der Unterseite des Fangs, Blesse am Kopf und weiße Unterseite des Körpers, welche, von einer horizontalen Linie in Ellenbogenhöhe an gemessen, sich bis zu einer Länge von 10 cm (4 Inches) ausdehnen darf.

Weiß am Kopf soll nicht vorherrschen, und die Augen sollen vollständig von Farbe und Pigment umgeben sein. Es ist charakteristisch, dass bluemerle Hunde mit zunehmendem Alter dunkler werden.

GRÖSSE:

Widerristhöhe: Die bevorzugte Widerristhöhe ist 51-58 cm (20-23 Inches) für Rüden und 46-53 cm (18-21 Inches) für Hündinnen. Bei der Beurteilung der Größe ist die Qualität des Hundes wichtiger als eine leichte Abweichung von der Idealgröße.

FEHLER:

Jede Abweichung von den vorgenannten Punkten muss als Fehler angesehen werden, dessen Bewertung in genauem Verhältnis zum Grad der Abweichung stehen sollte und dessen Einfluss auf die Gesundheit und das Wohlbefinden des Hundes und seine Fähigkeit, die verlangte rassetypische Arbeit zu erbringen, zu beachten ist.

SCHWERE FEHLER:

- Stehohren oder Hängeohren
- Untypisches Haar

DISQUALIFIZIERENDE FEHLER :

- Aggressive oder übermäßig ängstliche Hunde
- Hunde, die deutlich physische Abnormalitäten oder Verhaltensstörungen aufweisen.
- Vorbiß. Rückbiß mit mehr als 1/8 inch (2.5 mm). Kontakverlust durch kurze zentrale Schneidezähne bei sonst korrektem Gebiss soll nicht als Vorbiß beurteilt werden; abgebrochene oder durch Unfall fehlende Zähne sollen nicht bestraft werden.
- Weiße Flecken am Körper, d.h. zwischen Widerrist und Rute und seitlich zwischen Ellenbogen und Hinterseite der Hinterläufe; dies ist gültig für alle Farben.

N.B.

- Rüden müssen zwei offensichtlich normal entwickelte Hoden aufweisen, die sich vollständig im Hodensack befinden.
- Zur Zucht sollen ausschließlich funktional und klinisch gesunde, rassetypische Hunde verwendet werden.

Standard Nr. 367

Miniature American Shepherd (Miniatur Amerikanischer Schäferhunde)

Übersetzung: Firma Skrivanek / Offizielle Originalsprache: En. Durch Den VDH Überprüft.
Ursprung: Vereinigte Staaten Von Amerika
Patronat: Ungarn.
Datum der Publikation des Gültigen Offiziellen Standards: 04.09.2019.
Verwendung: Hüte- und Wachhund.
Klassifikation FCI: Gruppe 1 Hütehunde Und Treibhunde (Ausgenommen Schweizer Sennenhunde) Sektion 1 Schäferhunde. Ohne Arbeitsprüfung.

KURZER GESCHICHTLICHER ABRISS: Der Miniature American Shepherd entstand Ende der 1960er Jahre in Kalifornien aus den kleinen Australian Shepherds. Das Ziel der Züchtung war die Bewahrung ihrer geringen Größe, ihres lebhaften Charakters und ihrer Intelligenz.

1980 wurde die Rasse erstmals durch das National Stock Dog Registry registriert. Ursprünglich lautete die Bezeichnung Miniature Australian Shepherd. Zu Beginn der 1990er Jahre hatten die Hunde landesweit Popularität erlangt und wurde auf verschiedenen Treffen für seltene Rassen gezeigt. Der erste Zuchtverein und die Registrierung, MASCUSA, wurden 1990 gegründet und 1993 eingetragen. Im Mai 2011 wurde die Rasse als Miniature American Shepherd in das Rassebegründungsverfahren des AKC (USA) aufgenommen. Der Miniature American Shepherd Club of the USA (MASCUSA) ist eine Unterorganisation des designierten Dachverbandes American Kennel Club.

Die Rasse wurde zum Hüten kleiner Herden verwendet, wie Schafe und Ziege, hat jedoch auch die Fähigkeit größeres Vieh zu bewältigen. Ihre geringe Größe wurde als Vorteil erachtet, weil sie zusätzlich auch als Haustier gehalten werden konnte.

Als Begleiter von Reitern auf deren Weg zu Turnieren erlangten sie besondere Beliebtheit, weil ihre Intelligenz, Loyalität und Größe die Hunde zu einem hervorragenden Reisebegleiter machen. Auf diese Weise erlangten sie im gesamten Land Popularität.

Heute hat sich der Miniature American Shepherd in den USA und international etabliert. Es ist eine Rasse mit einer einzigartigen Identität - ein auffallender, vielseitiger kleiner Hütehund, der sich auf einer Ranch ebenso wohl fühlt wie in der Stadt.

ALLGEMEINES ERSCHEINUNGSBILD: Der Miniature American Shepherd ist ein kleiner Hütehund, der seinen Ursprung in den USA hat. Es ist etwas länger als hoch, von moderatem Knochenbau, Körpergröße und -höhe sind gut proportioniert, ohne Auffälligkeiten. Der Gang ist geschmeidig, leicht und balanciert. Seiner außergewöhnlichen Lebhaftigkeit, kombiniert mit Stärke und Ausdauer, verdankt er seine Eignung in unterschiedlichstem Gelände. Ein äußerst vielseitiger, energischer und ausdauernder Hund von herausragender Intelligenz und mit starker Hingabe zum Halter. Er ist sowohl ein loyaler Begleiter als auch ein gelehriger Arbeiter, worauf bereits sein aufmerksamer Ausdruck hinweist. Das Stockhaar ist von mittlerer Länge und Grobheit, von einheitlicher Farbe oder meliert, mit oder ohne weiße und/oder Loh (Kupfer) Abzeichen. Traditionell ist die Rute kupiert oder eine natürliche Stummelrute.

WICHTIGE PROPORTIONEN:

Gemessen vom Buggelenk bis zum Sitzbeinhöcker und vom höchsten Punkt des Schulterblatts bis zum Boden ist er etwas länger als hoch. Substanz - kräftig gebaut mit moderatem Knochenbau im Verhältnis zu Körperhöhe und -größe. Rüden strahlen Maskulinität aus, ohne grob zu wirken, Hündinnen erscheinen feminin, ohne zu leicht zu wirken. Die gesamte Struktur vermittelt einen Eindruck von Tiefe und Stärke, ohne jedoch massig zu wirken.

VERHALTEN/CHARAKTER (WESEN): Der intelligente Miniature American Shepherd ist primär ein Arbeitshund mit starkem Hüte- und Wachinstinkt. Er ist ein außergewöhnlicher Begleiter, vielseitig und gelehrig, der seine Aufgaben stilvoll und mit Begeisterung erledigt.

Fremden gegenüber ist er reserviert, jedoch nicht scheu. Er ist ein ausdauernder und robuster Arbeiter, der Verhalten und Auftreten seiner jeweiligen Aufgabe anpasst. In der Familie agiert er beschützend, freundlich, anhänglich und loyal.

KOPF:

OBERKOPF:

Schädel: Schädel - Das Schädeldach ist flach bis mäßig rund und kann einen leichten Hinterhauptstachel aufweisen. Breite und Länge des Schädeldachs sind identisch.

STOPP: Der Stopp ist mäßig, jedoch definiert ausgebildet.

GESICHTSSCHÄDEL:

NASENSCHWAMM: Rot Merle- und rote Hunde haben einen leberfarbenen Nasenspiegel Blau Merle- und schwarze Hunde haben ein schwarzes Nasenpigment. Voll pigmentierte Nasenschwämme werden bevorzugt. Nasenschwämme, die nicht vollständig pigmentiert sind, sind ein Fehler. Schwerer Fehler – 25 bis 50 Prozent fehlende Pigmentierung am Nasenspiegel.

FANG: Der Fang ist von mittlerer Breite und Tiefe, verjüngt sich graduell zu einer gerundeten Spitze, ohne schwer, quadratisch, spitz oder lose zu wirken. Die Länge entspricht der Länge des Oberkopfes . Flanken - Von der Seite gesehen sind Fang und Oberkopf leicht schräg zueinander angesetzt, wobei die Vorderseite der Krone einen leichten Winkel zum Nasenschwamm aufweist.

LEFZEN: Pigmentierung passend zur Farbe des Hundes, enganliegend.

KIEFER/ZÄHNE: Lückenloses Scherengebiss. Kein Punktabzug bei abgebrochenen, fehlenden oder verfärbten Zähnen infolge von Unfall. Disqualifikation: –Vor- oder Rückbiss.

AUGEN: Die Augen sind schräg angesetzt, mandelförmig, weder hervorstehend noch eingesunken und proportional zum Kopf. Akzeptabel in allen Fellfarben kann eines oder beide Augen braun, blau, haselnussbraun, bernsteinfarben oder jede Farbkombination davon aufweisen, einschließlich Tüpfel und Marmorierung.

Die Augenränder von roten und rotmelierten Tieren haben eine vollständige rote (leberbraune) Pigmentierung. Die Augenränder der schwarzen und blaumelierten Tiere weisen eine vollständige schwarze Pigmentierung auf. Die Blau merle und schwarzen Hunde weisen eine schwarze Augenumrandung auf, die Rot merle und roten Hunde zeigen eine leberfarbene (braune) Pigmentierung. Der Ausdruck ist aufgeweckt, aufmerksam und intelligent. Der Blick kann Fremden gegenüber reserviert oder aufmerksam sein.

OHREN: Dreieckig, von mäßiger Größe, am Kopf hoch angesetzt. Bei voller Aufmerksamkeit kippen sie nach vorne ab oder als Rosenohr zur Seite. Schwerer Fehler - Stehohren oder Hängeohren. .

HALS: Der Hals ist fest, sauber und proportional zum Körper. Er ist von mittlerer Länge und am Kamm leicht gebogen, mit gutem Übergang zur Schulterpartie.

KÖRPER: Der Körper ist fest und in guter Kondition.

OBERE LINIE: Der Rücken ist im Stand und in der Bewegung vom Widerrist zum Hüftgelenk fest und gerade.

WIDERRIST: Die Schulterblätter sind lang, flach, eng am Widerrist angesetzt und schräg.

RÜCKEN: Der Rücken ist im Stand und in der Bewegung fest und gerade vom Widerrist zum Hüftgelenk.

LENDEN: Die Lenden sind von oben gesehen stark und breit.

KRUPPE: Die Kruppe ist moderat abfallend.

BRUST: Die Brust ist voll und tief, bis zum Ellbogen reichend, mit gut gebogenen Rippen.

UNTERE PROFILLINIE UND BAUCH: Die untere Profillinie ist leicht aufgezogen.

RUTE: Eine kupierte oder natürliche Stummelrute wird bevorzugt. Die kupierte Rute ist gerade, nicht länger als 7,62 cm (3 Zoll) (in Ländern, in welchen dies gesetzlich nicht verboten ist).

Die nicht kupierte Rute kann in einer leichten Rundung herabhängen, wenn der Hund ruht. Bei Erregung oder in der Bewegung kann die Rute in einer ausgeprägten Rundung nach oben getragen werden.

GLIEDMASSEN

VORDERHAND:

ALLGEMEINES: Die Vorderhand ist gut konditioniert und ausgewogen zur Hinterhand gesetzt.

Vorderhand - Die Vorderhand fällt gerade und lotrecht zum Boden ab. Die Läufe sind gerade und stark. Der Knochen ist eher oval als rund.

SCHULTER: Die Schulterblätter sind lang, flach, eng am Widerrist angesetzt und schräg.

OBERARM: Die Länge des Oberarms (Oberarmknochen) ist mit der des Schulterblatts identisch und steht in einem nahezu rechten Winkel zum Schulterblatt.

ELLBOGEN: Das Ellbogengelenk ist vom Boden bis zum Widerrist abstandsgleich. Von der Seite gesehen sollte der Ellbogen direkt unter dem Widerrist sitzen. Ellbogen sollen eng an den Rippen anliegen, ohne locker zu sein.

UNTERARM: Die Läufe sind gerade und stark. Der Knochen ist eher oval als rund.

VORDERMITTELFUSS: Kurz, dick und stark, jedoch flexibel, von der Seite gesehen in einem leichten Winkel stehend.

Vorderpfoten: - Ovale, kompakte, feste, gut gewölbte Zehen. Die Ballen sind dick und elastisch, die Nägel sind kurz und stark. Die Nägel können jede Farbkombination aufweisen. Afterkrallen müssen entfernt werden (in Ländern, in welchen dies gesetzlich nicht verboten ist).

HINTERHAND:

ALLGEMEINES: Die Breite der Hinterhand erreicht ungefähr die Breite der Vorderhand an den Schultern. Winkelung - die Winkelung von Becken und Oberschenkel (Oberschenkelknochen) spiegelt die Winkelung von Schulterblatt und Oberarm wider; es wird ungefähr ein rechter Winkel gebildet.

OBERSCHENKEL: Der Oberschenkel ist gut bemuskelt, jedoch nicht übermäßig.

KNIE: Das Knie ist klar definiert.

SPRUNGGELENK: Die Sprunggelenke sind kurz, mäßig gewinkelt, so dass der Hintermittelfuß lotrecht zum Boden steht.

HINTERMITTELFUSS: Die Hintermittelfüße sind kurz, von der Seite gesehen lotrecht zum Boden und sie stehen von hinten gesehen parallel zueinander.

HINTERPFOTEN: Die Pfoten sind oval, mit kompakten, festen, gut gewölbten Zehen. Die Ballen sind dick und elastisch, die Nägel sind kurz und stark. Die Nägel können jede Farbkombination aufweisen. Afterkrallen müssen entfernt werden (in Ländern, in welchen dies gesetzlich nicht verboten ist).

GANGWERK: Der Gang ist fließend, frei, leicht und geschmeidig, mit einem gut ausgewogenen, raumgreifenden Schritt. Die Vorder- und die Hinterläufe bewegen sich gerade und parallel zur Mittellinie des Körpers. Bei größerer Geschwindigkeit bewegen sich die Vorder- und Hinterläufe in einer Konvergenz zum Schwerpunkt des Tieres, wobei der Rücken fest und gerade bleibt. Im Trab wird der Kopf in seiner natürlichen Position getragen, wobei der Hals sich nach Vorne verlängert und der Kopf nahezu in einer Linie zur Rückenlinie oder geringfügig darüber getragen wird. Der Hund muss in der Bewegung flink und fähig sein, augenblicklich einen Richtungswechsel vorzunehmen oder eine andere Gangart einzuschlagen.

HAUT: Die Haut ist von typischer mäßiger Dicke und Nachgiebigkeit.

HAARKLEID: Das Haarkleid vermittelt insgesamt einen moderaten Eindruck. Das Haar ist von mittlerer Struktur, gerade bis wellig, wetterfest und von mittlerer Länge. Der Anteil des Unterhaares variiert abhängig von den klimatischen Bedingungen.

HAAR: Am Kopf und an den Vorderseiten der Läufe ist das Haar kurz und glatt. Die Hinterseiten der Vorderläufe und die Hosen sind moderat befedert. Bei Rüden sind Mähne und Kragen moderat und ausgeprägter als bei Hündinnen. Das Haar kann an den Ohren, Pfoten, Rückseite der Sprunggelenke, Hintermittelfüßen und an der Rute getrimmt werden, sonst muss es als natürliches Haarkleid getragen werden. Ungetrimmte Tasthaare werden bevorzugt. Schwerer Fehler - Nicht typisches Haarkleid.

FARBE:

KÖRPERFARBE: Die Farbgebung bietet Variabilität und Individualität. Ohne Präferenzen sind die anerkannten Farben Blue merle, schwarz, Red. merle, rot Schwarz, Blue merle, Rot, Leberbraun und Red merle oder Leberbraun merle. Die Merlefarbgebung erscheint in jeder Ausprägung, Marmorierung, gefleckt oder als Sprenkel. Die Unterwolle kann etwas heller sein als das Deckhaar. Asymmetrische Abzeichen sind kein Fehler.

Lohfarbene Abzeichen: Lohfarbene Abzeichen sind nicht erforderlich, werden jedoch in allen der folgenden Bereiche akzeptiert: Um die Augen, an Pfoten, Läufen, Brust, Nasenschwamm, Halsunterseite, Gesicht, Ohrunterseite, untere Profillinie

des Körpers, unter der Rutenwurzel und an den Hosen. Lohfarbene Abzeichen variieren in Schattierungen von creme Beige bis dunkler Rost, ohne Präferenzen. Übergang in die Grundfarbe oder das Merle-Muster im Gesicht, an den Läufen, Pfoten und Hosen.

WEISSE ABZEICHEN: Weiße Abzeichen sind nicht erforderlich, dürfen ggf. jedoch nicht dominieren. Stichelung in den weißen Abzeichen ist erlaubt. Das Weiß ist am Kopf nicht vorherrschend und die Augen sind vollständig von Farbe und Pigmentierung umgeben. Rot Merle - und rote Hunde haben rote (lederbraunen) Pigmentierungen an den Augenrändern.

Blue Merle und schwarze Hunde haben schwarze Pigmentierung an den Augenrändern. Bevorzugt werden vollständig von Farbe bedeckte Ohren. Weiße Abzeichen in jeder Kombination und begrenzt auf Fang, Backen, Krone, Blesse auf dem Schädel, am Hals in einem Teil- oder Vollkragen, an Brust, Bauch, Vorderläufen und Hinterläufen bis zum Sprunggelenk und mit einem dünnen Ausläufer bis zum Knie. Ein geringer Anteil Weiß von der unteren Profillinie kann von der Seite sichtbar sein, darf jedoch nicht mehr als 2,5 cm (1 Zoll) über den Ellbogen reichen. Die Haarlinie des weißen Kragens reicht nicht über den Widerrist an der Haut hinaus. Die Spitze einer natürlichen, nicht kupierten Rute kann Weiß enthalten.

GRÖSSE UND GEWICHT:

WIDERRISTHÖHE:

Rüden: 35,5 cm bis zu 46 cm

Hündinnen: 33 cm bis zu einschließlich 43,5 cm

Gewicht: Ein gesundes Gewicht wird auf der individuellen Größe, dem Geschlecht und der Substanz basieren.

FEHLER: Jede Abweichung von den vorgenannten Punkten muss als Fehler angesehen werden, dessen Bewertung in genauem Verhältnis zum Grad

der Abweichung stehen sollte und dessen Einfluss auf die Gesundheit und das Wohlbefinden des Hundes zu beachten ist.

SCHWERE FEHLER:

• Nicht typische Haarkleider.

• Stehohren oder Hängeohren.

• Zwischen 25 und 50 Prozent pigmentierter Nasenspiegel

• Weiße Abzeichen, die mehr als 25 Prozent eines Ohres bedecken.

DISQUALIFIZIERENDE FEHLER:

• Aggressive oder übermäßig ängstliche Hunde.

Hunde, die deutlich physische Abnormitäten oder Verhaltensstörungen aufweisen.

• Unter 35,5 cm und über 46 cm für Rüden; unter 33 cm und über 43,5 cm für Hündinnen. Die im Rassestandard festgelegten Mindesthöhen gelten nicht für Rüden oder Hündinnen mit einem Alter unter sechs Monaten.

• Mehr als 50 Prozent fehlende Pigmentierung am Nasenspiegel.

• Vor- oder Rückbiss

• Andere als die anerkannten Farben. Weiße Körpersprenkel, das heißt, auffälliger, isolierter weißer Fleck oder Platte im Bereich zwischen Widerrist und Rute, auf dem Rücken oder an den Seiten zwischen den Ellbogen und der Hinterseite der Hinterläufe.

N.B.:

• Rüden müssen zwei offensichtlich normal entwickelte Hoden aufweisen, die sich vollständig im Hodensack befinden.

• Zur Zucht sollen ausschließlich funktional und klinisch gesunde, rassetypische Hunde zugelassen werden.

Recommendations for Judges

PROPORTIONS

- Moderation is important while maintaining breed type and breed typical head / expression – but it does not mean mediocre!
- Moderation means the elimination or reduction of extremes.
- Remember: slightly longer than tall – correct body length to height ratio is 10:9.
- Size: Aussies come in a wide range of sizes with no disqualification; choose based on functionality rather than size. Height is a disqualifing fault for MAS.
- Avoid rewarding dogs that have incorrect proportions and movement.
- Do not reward long and low, which diminishes stamina.

MOVEMENT

- Moderation of movement is very important. These breeds need the stamina to work all day.
- Smooth, free and easy, well-balanced with a ground-covering stride. They are light on their feet, exhibiting little or no effort. Balance is important! Coming, going and sidegait are all equally important.
- Look for fit dogs in good weight and muscle tone.
- Excessive speed and stringing up the dogs while gaiting should not be rewarded.

HEAD

- Look for typical keen expression and correct head details. Large, heavy ears and loose lips are not desireable.

GROOMING

- Excessive grooming should be not rewarded. If you can see scissoring marks or straight cut lines on the hair it is too much grooming. The dogs should be exhibited in a natural way. Trimming ears, feet, hocks and tail is acceptable; scissoring on the body is incorrect for these natural working breeds.

TYPE

- You will find a lot of variation in breed type – which is fine for these breeds.

ATTITUDE

- Not all Aussies and MAS love the show ring. Your best quality dog may not be the the most animated one. Select for quality over showmanship.

COLOUR

- Colouration and markings can create optical illusions, so when in doubt use your hands to examine.

Assymetric markings on legs and chest can trick the eye. When in doubt use your hands to examine.

Australian Shepherd

ORIGIN: United States of America.
DATE OF PUBLICATION of the Official Valid Standard: 26.03.2009.
UTILIZATION: Farm and ranch shepherd dog.
CLASSIFICATION F.C.I.: Group 1 Sheepdogs and Cattle dogs (except Swiss Cattle dogs) Section 1 Sheepdogs without working trial

BRIEF HISTORICAL SUMMARY:

While there are many theories as to the origin of the Australian Shepherd, the breed as we know it today developed exclusively in the United States. The Australian Shepherd was given its name because of the association with Basque Sheepherders who came to the United States from Australia in the 1800's.

The Australian Shepherd's popularity rose steadily with the boom of western horseback riding after World War II, which became known to the general public via rodeos, horse shows, movies, and television shows. Their inherent versatile and trainable personality made them assets to American farms and ranches. The American stockman continued the development of the breed, maintaining its versatility, keen intelligence, strong herding instincts, and eye-catching appearance that originally won their admiration.

Although each individual is unique in colour and markings, all Australian Shepherds show an unsurpassed devotion to their families. Their many attributes have guaranteed the Australian Shepherd's continued popularity.

GENERAL APPEARANCE:

The Australian Shepherd is well balanced, slightly longer than tall, of medium size and bone, with colouring that offers variety and individuality. He is attentive and animated, lithe and agile, solid and muscular without cloddiness. He has a coat of moderate length and coarseness. He has a docked or natural tail.

IMPORTANT PROPORTIONS:

Measuring from the breastbone to rear of thigh and from top of the withers to the ground the Australian Shepherd is slightly longer than tall. Solidly built with moderate bone. Structure in the male reflects masculinity without coarseness. Bitches appear feminine without being slight of bone.

BEHAVIOUR/TEMPERAMENT:

The Australian Shepherd is an intelligent working dog of strong herding and guarding instincts. He is a loyal companion and has the stamina to work all day. With an even disposition, he is good natured, seldom quarrelsome. He may be somewhat reserved in initial meetings.

HEAD: The head is clean cut, strong and dry. Overall size should be in proportion to the body.

CRANIAL REGION: SKULL: Top flat to slightly domed. It may show a slight occipital protuberance. Length and width are equal.

STOP: Moderate, well-defined.

FACIAL REGION:

NOSE: Blue merles and blacks have black pigmentation on the nose (and lips). Red merles and reds have liver (brown) pigmentation on the nose (and lips). On the merles it is permissible to have small pink spots; however, they should not exceed 25 % of the nose on dogs over one year of age, which is a SERIOUS FAULT.

MUZZLE: Equal in length or slightly shorter than the back skull. Viewed from the side the topline of the back skull and muzzle form parallel planes, divided by a moderate, well-defined stop. The muzzle tapers little from base to nose and is rounded at the tip.

JAWS/TEETH: A full complement of strong white teeth should meet in a scissors bite or may meet in a pincer bite.

EYES: Brown, blue, amber or any variation or combination thereof, including flecks and marbling. Almond shaped, not protruding nor sunken. The blue merles and blacks have black pigmentation on eye rims. The red merles and reds have liver (brown) pigmentation on eye rims.

EXPRESSION: Showing attentiveness and intelligence, alert and eager. Gaze should be keen but friendly.

EARS: Triangular, of moderate size and leather, set high on the head. At full attention they break forward and over, or to the side as a rose ear.

NECK: Strong, of moderate length, slightly arched at the crest, fitting well into the shoulders.

BODY:

TOP LINE: Back straight and strong, level and firm from withers to hip joints.

CROUP: Moderately sloping.

CHEST: Not broad, but deep with the lowest point reaching the elbow. Ribs: Well sprung and long, neither barrel chested nor slab-sided.

UNDERLINE AND BELLY: Shows a moderate tuck-up.

TAIL: Straight, naturally long or naturally short. When docked (in countries where this practice is not forbidden), or naturally short, not to exceed 10 cm.

LIMBS - FOREQUARTERS:

SHOULDER: Shoulder-blades long, flat, fairly close set at the withers and well laid back. The upper arm, which should be relatively the same length as the shoulder-blade, attaches at an approximate right angle to the shoulder line with forelegs dropping straight, perpendicular to the ground.

LEGS: Straight and strong. Bone strong, oval rather than round.

METACARPUS (Pastern): Medium length and very slightly sloping. Front dewclaws may be removed.

FOREFEET: Oval, compact, with close-knit, well-arched toes. Pads thick and resilient.

HINDQUARTERS:

GENERAL APPEARANCE: The width of the hindquarters is equal to the width of the forequarters at the shoulders.

ANGULATION of the pelvis and upper thigh corresponds to the angulation of the shoulder-blade and upper arm, forming an approximate right angle

STIFLE: Clearly defined.

HOCK JOINTS: Moderately bent. Hocks: Short, perpendicular to the ground and parallel to each other when viewed from the rear. No rear dewclaws.

HIND FEET: Oval, compact with close-knit, well-arched toes. Pads thick and resilient.

GAIT: The Australian Shepherd has a smooth, free and easy gait. He exhibits great agility of movement with a well-balanced, ground covering stride. Fore- and hind legs move straight and parallel with the centre line of the body. As speed increases, the feet (front and rear) converge toward the centre line of gravity of the dog while the back remains firm and level. The Australian Shepherd must be agile and able to change direction or alter gait instantly.

COAT:

HAIR: Of medium texture, straight to wavy, weather resistant and of medium length. The undercoat varies in quantity with variations in climate. Hair is short and smooth on the head, ears, front of forelegs and below the hocks. Backs of forelegs and breeches are moderately feathered. There is a moderate mane and frill, more pronounced in dogs than in bitches.

COLOUR: Blue merle, black, red merle, red – all with or without white markings and/or tan markings, with no order of preference.

HAIRLINE of a white collar does not exceed the point of the withers at the skin.

WHITE is acceptable on the neck (either in part or as a full collar), chest, legs, muzzle underparts, blaze on head and white extension from underpart up to four inches (10 cm), measuring from a horizontal line at the elbow. White on the head should not predominate, and the eyes must be fully surrounded by colour and pigment. Merles characteristically become darker with increasing age.

SIZE:

HEIGHT at the withers: The preferred height for males is 20-23 inches (51-58 cm), females 18-21 inches (46-53 cm). Quality is not to be sacrificed in favour of size.

FAULTS:

• Any departure from the foregoing points should be considered a fault and the seriousness with which the fault should be regarded should be in exact proportion to its degree and its effect upon the health and welfare of the dog.

SEVERE FAULTS:

• Prick ears and hanging ears.

• Non-typical coats.

DISQUALIFYING FAULTS:

• Aggressive or overly shy.

• Any dog clearly showing physical or behavioural abnormalities.

• Undershot. Overshot by more than 1/8 inch. Loss of contact caused by short center incisors in an otherwise correct bite shall not be judged undershot. Teeth broken or missing by accident shall not be penalized.

• White body splashes in all colours, which means white on body between withers and tail, on sides between elbows and back of hindquarters.

N.B. (Nota Bene: please note)

• Male animals should have two apparently normal testicles fully descended into the scrotum.

• Only functionally and clinically healthy dogs, with breed typical conformation, should be used for breeding.

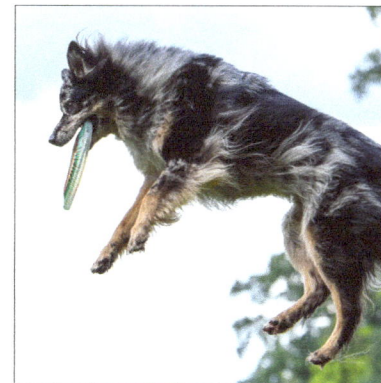

Miniature American Shepherd

ORIGIN: United States of America.
PATRONAGE: Hungary.
DATE OF PUBLICATION of the Official Valid Standard: 04/09/2019.
UTILIZATION: Farm and ranch shepherd dog.
FCI-CLASSIFICATION: Group 1 Sheepdogs and Cattledogs (except Swiss Cattledogs) Section 1 Sheepdogs. Without working trial.

BRIEF HISTORICAL SUMMARY:

The Miniature American Shepherd was developed in California during the late 1960's with the breeding of small Australian Shepherds. These dogs were bred with a goal of maintaining their small size, active character and intelligence. The breed was first registered with the National Stock Dog Registry in 1980 and was originally called the Miniature Australian Shepherd. By the early 1990's, they had attained nationwide popularity and were shown in various rare-breed organizations. The first parent breed club and registry, MASCUSA, was formed in 1990 and incorporated in 1993. The breed entered the AKC Foundation Stock Service as the Miniature American Shepherd in May 2011. The Miniature American Shepherd Club of the USA (MASCUSA) is the designated national parent club of the American Kennel Club.

The breed has been used for herding smaller stock such as sheep and goats, although they have the heart to tackle larger stock as well. Their small size was looked upon with favor, as they could more easily double as a household pet. They became especially popular with equestrians traveling to horse shows, as their intelligence, loyalty, and size made them an excellent travel companion. In this way their popularity spread across the country.

Today, the Miniature American Shepherd is established across the U.S. and internationally. It is a breed with a unique identity - an eye catching, versatile little herding dog, equally at home on a ranch or in the city.

GENERAL APPEARANCE:

The Miniature American Shepherd is a small size herding dog that originated in the United States. He is slightly longer than tall with bone that is moderate and in proportion to body size and height without extremes. Movement is smooth, easy, and balanced. Exceptional agility combined with strength and stamina allows for working over a variety of terrain. This highly versatile, energetic dog makes an excellent athlete with superior intelligence and a willingness to please those to whom he is devoted. He is both a loyal companion and a biddable worker, which is evident in his watchful expression. The double coat of medium length and coarseness may be solid in colour or merled, with or without white and/or tan (copper) markings. He traditionally has a docked or natural bobtail.

IMPORTANT PROPORTIONS:

Measuring from the point of the shoulder to the point of the buttocks and from the highest point of the shoulder blade to the ground, he is slightly longer than tall. Substance - Solidly built with moderate bone in proportion to body height and size. Structure in the dog reflects masculinity without coarseness. bitches appear feminine without being slight of bone. The overall structure gives an impression of depth and strengt without bulkiness.

BEHAVIOUR/TEMPERAMENT:

The Miniature American Shepherd is intelligent, primarily a working dog of strong herding and guardian instincts. An exceptional companion, he is versatile and easily trained, performing his assigned tasks with great style and enthusiasm. Although reserved with strangers, he does not exhibit shyness. He is a resilient and persistent worker, who adjusts his demeanor and arousal appropriately to the task at hand. With his family he is protective, good natured, devoted and loyal.

HEAD:

CRANIAL REGION: SKULL: The crown is flat to slightly round and may show a slight occipital protuberance. The width and the length of the crown are equal.

STOP: The stop is moderate but defined.

FACIAL REGION:

NOSE: Red merles and reds have red (liver) pigmentation on the nose leather. Blue merles and blacks have black pigmentation on the nose leather. Fully pigmented noses are preferred.

NOSES that are less than fully pigmented will be FAULTED.

SEVERE FAULT – 25 to 50 percent unpigmented nose leather.

MUZZLE: The muzzle is of medium width and depth and tapers gradually to a rounded tip without appearing heavy, square, snipy, or loose. Length is equal to the length of the crown. Planes - Viewed from the side, the muzzle and the top line of the crown are slightly oblique to each other, with the front of the crown on a slight angle downward toward the nose

LIPS: pigment to match colour of dog, to be tight fitting.

JAWS/TEETH: A full complement of teeth meet in a scissor bite. Teeth broken, missing or discoloured by accident are not penalized.

DISQUALIFICATION - Undershot or overshot bite.

EYES: The eyes are set obliquely, almond shaped, neither protruding nor sunken and in proportion to the head. Acceptable in all coat colours, one or both eyes may be brown, blue, hazel, amber or any colour combination thereof, including flecks and marbling. The eye rims of the reds and red merles have full red (liver) pigmentation. The eye rims of the blacks and blue merles have full black pigmentation. The expression is alert, attentive, and intelligent. They may express a reserved look or be watchful of strangers.

EARS: Are triangular, of moderate size, set high on the head. At full attention they break forward and over, or to the side as a rose ear.

SEVERE FAULT - Prick ears and ears that hang with no lift.

NECK: The neck is firm, clean, and in proportion to the body. It is of medium length and slightly arched at the crest, fitting well into the shoulders.

BODY: The body is firm and well-conditioned

TOP LINE: The back is firm and level from the withers to the hip joint when standing or moving.

WITHERS: Shoulder blades (scapula) are long, flat, fairly close set at the withers, and well laid back.

BACK: The back is firm and level from the withers to the hip joint when standing or moving.

LOIN: The loin is strong and broad when viewed from the top.

CROUP: The croup is moderately sloped.

CHEST: The chest is full and deep, reaching to the elbow, with well sprung ribs.

UNDERLINE AND BELLY: The underline show a moderate tuck-up.

TAIL: A docked or natural bobtail is preferred. A docked tail is straight, not to exceed three (3) inches (in countries where it is not forbidden by law). The undocked tail when at rest may hang in a slight curve. When excited or in motion the tail may be carried raised with the curve accentuated.

LIMBS - FOREQUARTERS:

GENERAL APPEARANCE: The forequarters are well conditioned and balanced with the hindquarters.

FORELEGS: The forelegs drop straight and perpendicular to the ground. The legs are straight and strong. The bone is oval rather than round.

SHOULDER: Shoulder blades (scapula) are long, flat, fairly close set at the withers, and well laid back.

UPPER ARM: The upper arm (humerus) is equal in length to the shoulder blade and meets the shoulder blade at an approximate right angle.

ELBOW: The elbow joint is equidistant from the ground to the withers. Viewed from the side, the elbow should be directly under the withers. The elbows should be close to the ribs without looseness.

FOREARM: The legs are straight and strong. The bone is oval rather than round.

METACARPUS (pastern): Short, thick and strong, but still flexible, showing a slight angle when viewed from the side.

FOREFEET: Oval shaped, compact, with close-knit, well-arched toes. Pads are thick and resilient; nails are short and strong. The nails may be any colour combination. Dewclaws should be removed (except where it is forbidden by law).

HINDQUARTERS:

GENERAL APPEARANCE: Width of hindquarters is approximately equal to the width of the forequarters at the shoulders. Angulation - The angulation of the pelvis and upper thigh (femur) mirrors the angulation of the shoulder blade and upper arm, forming an approximate right angle.

THIGH: The thigh is well muscled, but not overly so.

STIFLE (knee): Stifles are clearly defined.

HOCK JOINT: The hocks are short, moderately bent to allow the metatarsal to fall perpendicular to the ground.

METATARSUS (Rear pastern): The metatarsals are short, perpendicular to the ground when viewed from the side and parallel to each other when viewed from the rear.

HIND FEET: Feet are oval, compact, with close knit, well arched toes. Pads are thick and resilient; nails are short and strong. The nails may be any colour combination. Rear dewclaws should be removed (in countries where it is not forbidden by law).

GAIT / MOVEMENT: The gait is smooth, free and easy exhibiting agility of movement with a well-balanced, ground-covering stride. The fore and hind legs move straight and parallel with the center line of the body; as speed increases, the feet, both front and rear, converge toward the center line of gravity of the dog while the back remains firm and level. When traveling at a trot, the head is carried in a natural position with the neck extended forward and head nearly level or slightly above the topline. He must be agile and able to turn direction or alter gait instantly.

SKIN: Skin is of typical moderate thickness and laxiety.

COAT: Moderation is the overall impression of the coat. Hair is of medium texture, straight to wavy, weather resistant, and of medium length. The undercoat varies in quantity with variations in climate.

HAIR: Hair is short and smooth on the head and front of the legs. The backs of forelegs and breeches are moderately feathered. There is a moderate mane and frill, more pronounced in dogs than in bitches. Hair may be trimmed on the ears, feet, back of hocks, pasterns, and tail, otherwise he is to be shown in a natural coat. Untrimmed whiskers are preferred.

SEVERE FAULT: Non-typical coats.

COLOUR:

BODY COLOUR: The colouring offers variety and individuality. With no order of preference, the recognized colours are black, blue merle, red, liver and red or liver merle. The merle will exhibit in any amount, marbling, flecks or blotches. Undercoats may be somewhat lighter in colour than the topcoat. Asymmetrical markings are not to be faulted.

TAN MARKINGS: Tan markings are not required but when present are acceptable in any or all of the following areas: around the eyes, on the feet, legs, chest, muzzle, underside of neck, face, underside of ear, underline of body, under the base of the tail and the breeches. Tan markings vary in shades from creamy beige to dark rust, with no preference. Blending with the base colour or merle pattern may be present on the face, legs, feet, and breeches.

WHITE MARKINGS: White markings are not required but when present do not dominate. Ticking may be present in white markings. White on the head does not predominate, and the eyes are fully surrounded by colour and pigment. Red merles and reds have red (liver) pigmentation on the eye rims. Blue merles and blacks have black pigmentation on the eye rims.

EARS fully covered by colour are preferred.

White markings may be in any combination and are restricted to the muzzle, cheeks, crown, blaze on head, the neck in a partial or full collar, chest, belly, front legs, hind legs up the hock and may extend in a thin outline of the stifle. A small amount of white extending from the underline may be visible from the side, not to exceed one inch above the elbow.

HAIRLINE of a white collar does not exceed the withers at the skin. If a natural UNDOCKED TAIL is present, the tip of the tail may have white.

SIZE AND WEIGHT:

HEIGHT AT THE WITHERS:

MALES: 35.5 cm up to 46 cm at the top of the withers

FEMALES: 33 cm up to and including 43.5 cm at the top of the withers.

WEIGHT: Healthy weight will vary based on individual size, sex and substance.

FAULTS:

Any departure from the foregoing points should be considered a fault and the seriousness with which the fault is regarded should be in exact proportion to its degree and its effect upon the health and welfare of the dog and its ability to perform its traditional work.

SEVERE FAULTS:

- Non-typical coats.
- Prick ears and ears that hang with no lift.
- Between 25 and 50% unpigmented nose leather
- White markings covering over 25% of an ear

DISQUALIFYING FAULTS:

- Aggressive or extremely shy dogs.
- Any dog clearly showing physical or behavioral abnormalities.
- Under 35.5 cm and over 46 cm for dogs; under 33 cm and over 43.5 cm for bitches. The minimum heights set forth in this Breed Standard shall not apply to dogs or bitches under six months of age.
- Over 50 percent unpigmented nose leather.
- Undershot or overshot bite.
- Other than recognized colours.
- White body splashes, which means any conspicuous, isolated spot or patch of white on the area between withers and tail, on back, or sides between elbows and back of hindquarters.

N.B. (Nota Bene: please note)

- Male animals should have two apparently normal testicles fully descended into the scrotum.
- Only functionally and clinically healthy dogs, with breed typical conformation should be used for breeding.

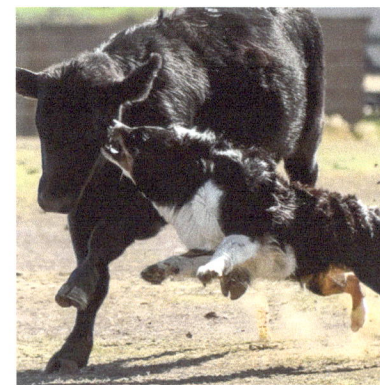

Paula McDermid
Author and Designer
Australian Shepherd Club of America breeder-judge licensed in 1986. American Kennel Club breeder-judge licensed in 1995. Australian Shepherd Club of America Hall of Fame Kennel "Bainbridge" established in 1980. Breeder of Best in Specialty Show and Group winners, National Specialty Most Versatile Aussie award-winner, and nationally top-ranked Aussie in agility. Licensed to judge nine American Kennel Club breeds. Former Vice President and board member of the United States Australian Shepherd Association. Author of books about Australian Shepherds.

Claudia Bosselmann
Collaborator
Breeder of Australian Shepherds since 2002 under the "Rafter Creek" kennel name. Licensed by the FCI to judge Australian Shepherds in 2012 and Miniature American Shepherds in 2019. President of the Club für Australian Shepherd Germany for 20 years; this club has also been responsible for the Miniature American Shepherd in Germany since 2019. Bred and owned FCI Worldwinner, FCI Jahrhundertsieger, VDH Bundessieger, VDH Europasieger, multiple Champions, and German Champion Obedience. Licensed by the FCI to also judge Siberian Huskies, Alaskan Malamutes, Islandic Sheepdogs, Lapinkoira, and Samoyed. Author of books about Australian Shepherds.

Inga Cerbule
Collaborator
Imported the first Australian Shepherds to the Baltic States in 1994. Established the Australian Shepherd kennel "Sentikki" in 1998. Licensed by the FCI to judge Australian Shepherds in 2017. Licensed by the FCI to judge Miniature American Shepherds in 2019. Licensed by the FCI to judge 24 Herding breeds. Owned or bred World Winners, European Winners, Best in Show and Group winners. Secretary of the FCI Breeding Commission, Board member of the Latvian Kennelclub (FCI). Lecturer at the Latvian University of Life Sciences, Veterinary Medicine program. Lecturer at the Latvian Kennel Club, Continuing Education Program for judges and breeders.

Paula McDermid
Autor und Designer
Australian Shepherd Club of America Züchter und Richter lizenziert 1986. American Kennel Club Züchter und Richter lizenziert 1995. Australian Shepherd Club of America Hall of Fame Kennel „Bainbridge", gegründet 1980. Züchter von Best In Specialty Show und Gruppensiegern, National Specialty Most Versatile Sieger und national hochplatzierte Aussies in Agility. Zugelassen, um neun American Kennel Club Rassen zu richten. Ehemalige Vizepräsidentin und Vorstandsmitglied der Australian Shepherd Association der Vereinigten Staaten. Autor von Büchern über Australian Shepherds.

Claudia Bosselmann
Mitarbeiter
Züchter von Australian Shepherds seit 2002 unter dem Zwingernamen „Rafter Creek". Von der FCI lizenziert, 2012 Australian Shepherds und 2019 Miniature American Shepherds zu richten. 20 Jahre Präsident des Club für Australian Shepherd Deutschland; dieser Verein ist seit 2019 auch für den Miniature American Shepherd in Deutschland verantwortlich. Gezüchtet und Besessen FCI Worldwinner, FCI Jahrhundertsieger, VDH Bundessieger, VDH Europasieger, mehrfache Champions und German Champion Obedience. Von der FCI lizenziert, um auch Siberian Huskies, Alaskan Malamutes, Islandic Sheepdogs, Lapinkoira und Samojeden zu richten. Autor von Büchern über Australian Shepherds.

Inga Cerbule
Mitarbeiter
Hat 1994 die ersten Australian Shepherds in die baltischen Staaten importiert. 1998 hat sie den Australian Shepherd Zwinger Sentikki gegründet. Im Jahr 2017 wurde sie von der FCI lizenziert um Australian Shepherds zu richten, in 2019 Miniature American Shepherd. Von der FCI lizenziert um weitere 24 Hütehunderassen zu richten. Gezüchtet oder besessen: Weltsieger, Europasieger, Best in Show- und Gruppensieger. Sekretär der FCI-Zuchtkommission, Vorstandsmitglied des Lettischen Kennelclubs (FCI). Dozent an der Lettischen Universität für Biowissenschaften, Studiengang Veterinärmedizin Dozent beim Lettischen Kennel Club, Weiterbildungsprogramm für Richter und Züchter.

www.ingramcontent.com/pod-product-compliance
Lightning Source LLC
Chambersburg PA
CBHW041552030426

42336CB00004B/50